A TEACHER'S GUIDE TO
USING PORTRAITS

Susan Morris

English ✤ Heritage

CONTENTS

4. Miss Brummell, by Gainsborough (detail).

ABOUT THIS BOOK

Portraits are the gossip columns, newsflashes, party political broadcasts and family albums of the past – of the age before photography, radio, television, modern printing techniques, computers and all the host of other technologies which record and transmit images or ideas today. If you were Queen Elizabeth I, how would you ensure that the far-flung subjects who would never see you knew to whom they owed their allegiance, unless by their seeing the royal portrait in a great house, on a coin or on an illuminated document? If you were the Earl of Monmouth, how would you record a major career success such as appointment to a position in a royal household? How could the birth of an heir be commemorated? How would lovers remember each other when separated?

The answer is that an artist was found and commissioned to produce, by hand, the required image. Later the development of reliable, relatively

cheap photography (c1850) meant that such needs could be fulfilled without a hand-made portrait; thus artists became interested in portraits which were more abstract, more experimental and less photographic.

Portraits are therefore a bubbling mass of pent-up emotions, events, comments and personalities. The problem is using them.

The purpose of this book is to help decode some of the messages to be found in portraits. The first chapters aim at helping general understanding, and then later there are suggestions for practical activities for groups. Because it is important that teachers feel confident enough to do for themselves what they ask of their groups, there are questions and exercises scattered throughout with suggested responses where appropriate. These are the highly subjective responses of the author but give an idea of the range of material that can be drawn from portraits.

6. Unknown child in photographer's studio, c1890.

5. Typical examples of portraits found in public and private collections. Mary Finch, Viscountess Andover, painted by Thomas Hudson in the 1740s.

In this book the word 'portrait' is used to mean a work for which there was a consciously posed sitting by a person or a group, and in which the sitter's identity is the main object of study. This is to distinguish portraits from, firstly, pictures of people where no real person's identity is central to the purpose (such as figure studies, where the artist is practising drawing skills, or 'story' pictures, often called genre pictures) and, secondly, from snapshot-like images where the person's likeness is captured unannounced, without prior posing of any sort. The distinctions are difficult and capable of much argument, but for clarity it will help to try to maintain them.

With regard to style and media, information and activities based on abstracts, caricatures, photography and sculpture are included. Moving images such as video or cinematography are not. Techniques of production have not been covered in detail.

TALKING TO THE WALL

There is a considerable difference between casually looking at something and visually studying it. In the first, the eyes are apparently focussed on an object or scene; in the second, the eyes are not only focussed but the brain is also active, registering and pondering what is seen. Think how much you 'see' without consciously registering any of it. On a school visit, the point is important because it is the difference between the pupils dutifully casting their gaze over the prescribed exhibits or critically registering what is in front of them. It is particularly easy to survey portraits without seeing them because the human form is quickly recognised, dismissed as ordinary and then forgotten.

The purpose of this chapter is to suggest to teachers a way of activating a response so that the portraits become less like wallpaper and more intrinsically dynamic. From this more exciting state, a multitude of activities can spring. The method is based on a simple assumption: that both sitter and artist were generally trying to reveal something about themselves when they arrived at the chosen form of the portrait.

Whoever the sitter in a portrait was, the decision to sit suggests that he or she was content to see something about himself/herself recorded. That something might have been becoming queen or being knighted, pride in a beautiful face or the birth of twins, or the desire for a picture for a lover to keep.

Imagine looking at your own family album. Probably every picture of yourself can be introduced by 'this was when I . . .': when you were born, when you reached your first birthday, ran in the school sports, were in the school play, went to Jo's wedding and so on. Rarely is a picture made for absolutely no reason at all. But even without help from you, most people looking at your album today will recognise effortlessly the subtle variety of clothes, objects or scenes which signify 'relay race', 'party clothes' or 'wedding reception'.

Based on these two principles – that there is generally a reason for the production of a portrait and that it will include information about the sitter and/or occasion – you can look at any portrait with the certainty that it is not a dumb, closed, meaningless item, but that it represents a set of choices: a statement is being made to you, and your reaction is required.

The following is a simplified approach to help you develop the skill of decoding these choices and statements. It will accustom you to communicating with sitters even when you do not know who they are. Looking in turn at the decisions represented by the portrait's costume, facial expression, bodily pose or gesture, background and accessories, inscriptions, colours, size, medium and even the frame will all help the interpretation. Figurative portraits in which the natural, realistic human likeness of a single sitter is predominant are dealt with first, then caricatures and abstracts, and finally group portraits.

COSTUME

Someone intending to have their portrait recorded has usually to clothe themselves for the occasion. The outfit chosen can therefore be assumed to hold some significance for the sitter and to relate to the reason for having the portrait made.

Below are described some of the conventional outfits often seen in formal portraits and whose meaning is very revealing once you recognise them.

Ermine and coronet

peer/peeress of the realm, entitled to sit in the House of Lords.

LORD MANSFIELD,
Chief Justice of England

7. The robes of an earl. Note the ermine around the shoulders. The number of rows of black 'dots' in the ermine indicate the rank: four for a duke, three for an earl and so on.

Garter robes

8. Full Garter robes: plumed hat, red surcoat, blue cloak fastened by great tasselled cords, the Garter chain and George (pendant badge).

Knight of the Garter. The highest order of British knighthood, hence the wearer is announcing appropriate chivalric qualities of character and status. The monarch is head of the Order. Don't confuse Garter robes with coronation robes and be careful to recognise the implications of having chosen one or the other. Shown here is the full ceremonial outfit. In 'everyday' wear, the chain bearing the badge of St George killing the dragon, the Garter Star, or the garter itself with the motto *Honi soit qui mal y pense*, or a blue sash over the right shoulder could be worn. See also Figs 20 and 22.

Other honours, such as the Thistle or Order of the Bath, may also frequently be seen.

Coronation robes

great cloak lined with ermine, and the regalia. Here the wearer is emphasising the right to rule, rather than personal qualities such as kindness, intellect, etc.

Roman robes, toga, tunic, buskins, sandals	allusions to statesmanship, honourable character, military leadership.
Crown of laurels	*either* wisdom, intellectual strength, Poet Laureate *or* victory in battle.
Ecclesiastical robes, or robes of office, eg. chancellor, judge	again, the reference is to the status of the wearer or the qualities which enable him to hold that post. Peers', judges' and cardinals' robes are all scarlet: look for the cardinal's square red hat and lace apron, and the peer's ermine bands.

9. Judges' robes. The sitter was Lord Chief Justice. Note the white 'falling bands' at the neck and the formal wig.

10. The sitter is wearing the long black robes trimmed with rows of gold brocade on sleeves and hem which indicate important ministerial responsibility.

Loosely draped dresses, off the shoulder

sometimes worn by women when normal day dress was heavily corseted. Naturally, they draw attention to physical charms.

11. Catherine Sedley, Countess of Dorchester, as if appearing through her bed-curtains.

Soft turbans, shaven head

sometimes worn by men when normal public day dress was a heavy wig. Gentlemen wore these caps for comfort, at home, or with friends, thereby stressing their relaxed style. Suggests bohemianism, and men shown thus are nearly always writers, composers or artists wearing the dress of their creative moments. Shirts and cuffs are often undone a casual fashion in the same portraits.

12. This sitter's head is shown close-cropped; it would normally be hidden under a wig. Note, however, the loose clothing suggesting Roman robes. The bust is therefore implying classical virtue rather than casual informality.

High attention to costume detail	leader or follower of fashion; member of smart society. See Fig 21.
Colour	black can indicate piety, mourning, scholarliness, sobriety or a cleric; white can indicate a bride and virginity; many other colours evoke an instinctive response, for example, pink seems feminine, purple grand, yellow vivacious and so on.
Armour	obvious military connotations but need not indicate that actual fighting has taken place. Highly decorated armour was worn to tournaments at court, and indicates knightly refinement and chivalry. Full suits of armour were not used by fighting men in battle after c1485. Breastplates and thick leather jerkins were mostly used for fighting after that date.
Ring	part of the coronation regalia, or of the ceremony when a nun's vows are taken, and, since Anglo-Saxon times, a token of loyalty and service between master and man. Rings symbolise wealth as well as a relationship. Until fairly recently, wedding rings were commonly worn on any finger, not always, as now, on the left hand.

13. Along with his breastplate, the sitter wears an elegant lace cravat, some grand flowing drapes, and around his hips the suggestion of a Roman tunic skirt: in other words, not authentic fighting gear.

Exercise on costume
Study this portrait. What conclusions can you draw about the sitter from her clothing?

14.

Suggested response
The Duchess is drawing your attention to her aristocracy by the coronet on the cushion, and the robe trimmed with ermine. She is also displaying her famed beauty; note the loose, low-necked chemise undone at the bodice and her hair tumbling down around her shoulders. It's rather an odd combination, but probably intended to be provocative.

Notice that surprisingly, in the list of costumes given above, many are forms of dressing-up or fantasy, as opposed to everyday wear. Sitters can also wear strange combinations of clothes if they wish to make more than one point about themselves, for example, the Roman toga with the Garter Star. A high percentage of sitters dress as gods or goddesses, Greek philosophers, Turkish ladies, royalists, saints, shepherdesses and so on. It is always extremely interesting (and can be very revealing) to discover what roles individuals fancy for themselves. You may be witnessing aspects of their character which will not be recorded anywhere else!

15. Prince Alfred, Queen Victoria's second son, as 'Autumn', in part of a series of 'Tableaux of the seasons' by the royal children in 1854.

Aggressive · Agonized · Anxious · Apologetic · Arrogant · Bashful · Blissful

Bored · Covetous · Cold · Concentrating · Confident · Curious · Demure

Determined · Disappointed · Disapproving · Disbelieving · Disgusted · Distasteful · Eavesdropping

Ecstatic · Enraged · Envious · Exasperated · Exhausted · Frightened · Frustrated

Grieving · Guilty · Happy · Horrified · Hot · Hungover · Hurt

Hysterical · Indifferent · Idiotic · Innocent · Interested · Jealous · Joyful

Loaded · Lonely · Lovestruck · Meditative · Mischievous · Miserable · Negative

Obstinate · Optimistic · Pained · Paranoid · Perplexed · Prudish · Puzzled

Regretful · Relieved · Sad · Satisfied · Shocked · Sheepish · Smug

Surly · Suprised · Suspicious · Sympathetic · Thoughtful · Undecided · Withdrawn

EXPRESSION AND POSE

Once dressed and with the artist, the sitter will try to adopt an appropriately meaningful pose. Even where speedy photography is used, even where a natural, relaxed look is desired, it is necessary to pose. Sitters rarely present a totally blank face and body to the artist (unless, of course, that *is* the point they wish to make to the viewer). This stage is crucial and it can take several sessions to achieve the satisfaction of both artist and sitter.

The facial expression is very important to compose, because people identify and assess each other most readily by the face. If the portrait is only going to show part of a person, it's the body that will be omitted, not the face. Often it is *only* the face which is shown, and the artist's whole representation of the character of the person must be assumed to be contained in it. In making portraits, artists nearly always begin with the face before they work on any other part, because if the face doesn't work there's no point in going on.

Faces are very mobile, but face muscles are not strong enough to hold any one expression for long without rather disfiguring consequences. Try it. About the most that can be achieved is a slight tension or relaxation of brows and mouth. However, eyes can be directed to one spot indefinitely, and the combination of the set of the head with the direction of the eyes can be varied immensely. Try it: find as many positions for your head to hold as you can. In each, try moving your glance around: down your nose haughtily, up to the left dreamily, chin up aggressively, and so on. Add to this tension or relaxation of the brows and mouth and a vast gallery of expressions is possible.

When studying a portrait to see what expression, what facial alignments, have been chosen, remember that you will usually need to look quite studiously to savour what the expression offers. The longer you look, the more you will tend to see.

16. The many different configurations of the features show how much we can convey with our faces.

Exercise on facial expression

Study the expressions shown here. Then analyse what parts of the face have been composed to suggest the expression — eyes, brows, mouth, throat, forehead, angle of face. What personal characteristics are suggested to you by each face? Don't make a quick judgment.

Suggested responses

Munshi Hafiz's head is held erect but just slightly tilted off vertical and with the chin forward, giving him a confident, self-contained air, helped by the firmly closed lips and the distant, contemplative expression in the eyes. The right brow seems slightly raised, as if cynically, and this half of the face is thrown into shadow as if withdrawing from the viewer. The neatly trimmed beard and moustache and the handsome turban give the impression of

17.

18.

someone careful of his appearance. The wide curves of beard, lips, eyebrows and turban suggest a broad and steady character.

The Dutch gentleman's eyes appear to focus on the viewer and make much more direct contact. This effect is heightened by the smile and the

backward-thrown position of the head, which makes him seem to be in the middle of reacting to what was just said. Despite the elegant beard and collar the hair seems unkempt, and despite the smile, the eyes, with their droop at the outside corners, appear sad. He seems to be a complex, enigmatic character.

The sitter's body is similarly arranged in a significant way, and again needs to be studied slowly because often the small details — fingers, shoulder alignment, weight distribution — are the most potent ones. Does the sitter lean towards you, or retreat? Are the legs sturdily set or elegantly composed? We almost instinctively recognise the poses of basic body language which suggest to us that sitters have certain physical qualities or mental states — grace, confidence, grief, pride and so on. Seventeenth and eighteenth century artists and intellectuals produced books and essays illustrating ideals of pose for use as reference works. Often these also specified the poses of polite deportment for everyday life such as bowing, standing or walking. Bewigged eighteenth century gentlemen frequently adopt positions which to us look surprisingly silly, but were to them part of a system of graceful posture in both movement and repose. What rules of polite deportment affect your own movements today?

Just as there are symbolic colours

and symbolic outfits for particular types, there are some conventional poses for certain roles:

Finger to forehead or head resting on hand

philosopher, intellectual or author.

19. Alexander Pope in a pose which suitably expresses his role as poet and author.

Looking expectantly upward

again, a thinker or a writer in the moment of creative inspiration.

On horseback

imperial authority. The image dates back to the Roman emperors and was adopted by Christian kings.

The 'Apollo Belvedere'

20. John Stuart, 3rd Earl of Bute, in the heroic pose of the Apollo Belvedere. Note the positions of head, arms, legs, and look for it even in women's portraits.

the pose of a much admired classical statue, it represents physical strength and heroic status. There are other famous and traditional poses drawn from Greek and Roman statues, such as that of the 'dying Gaul', which artists might wish to refer to by recalling that specific pose. Similarly there are traditional group poses such as the triangular group of Mary, Joseph and baby Jesus, or that of the Deposition from the Cross.

Hand on hip

21. The pose of a tough man of action.

used by Elizabethans to indicate a man of action; tough and masculine. The bent arm keeps the cloak back so that the other arm can quickly bring the sword from the scabbard. Either arm could be bent although swords were worn on the left hip by right-handed fighters.

Gestures are a bolder form of pose which, if properly executed, make for a much livelier portrait and support even further the illusion that the sitter really lives in the portrait; thus they are the work of an ambitious artist.

An even subtler refinement is to pose the sitter so that movement seems expected at any second, for instance, that the sitter will turn back to his desk, stand up, mount the horse and so on. Unbalanced body weight or an acute turn of the torso creates this illusion. Implied bodily movement is greatly to be desired for portraits of runners, actors, dancers, soldiers.

Equally, perfect calm or stillness can be a high artistic achievement.

Some poses are related to contemporary clothing, and the changing concept of elegance relates to this historical aspect as well. For example, wigs restrict the ability to incline the head and body; Elizabethan farthingales make it natural to fold the hands tidily in front of the waist; padded trunks prevent crossed legs; eighteenth century corsets make the upper body stiffly inflexible and cause the head to be held very erect; Edwardian corsets produce the full-bosomed and full-bottomed S-profile; Regency starched cravats and collars cause the chin to be held very high.

Added to the inevitable consequences on pose of wearing certain garments, however, are other factors worth bearing in mind when studying a pose. One is the aesthetic effect: the contribution the pose makes to an attractive or compelling work of art. An extended arm or finger may direct your eye to another area of the composition, or add impact and drama to one part of it. The pose may echo or be echoed by other elements – features of the landscape, arrangements of colours – to make a meaningful link with them, or add rhythms to the appearance. The arrangement of groups can be made more harmonious by poses adopted for their aesthetic appeal. At certain periods the prevailing favoured design in other arts such as architecture or interior decor may also have an effect on the desired general appearance of the portrait, and hence on pose, clothes, backgrounds. For example, the baroque period (late seventeenth century in England) saw the use of flowing, dramatic curves on a grand scale, and the effect on pose is visible; similarly neo-classical architecture, with its narrower, cleaner lines, influenced portrait painters.

Exercise on pose

Study the poses of the sitters in these illustrations. What adjectives would you select to describe each sitter? Can you analyse what, specifically, in each pose causes your response?

Suggested reponse

The sitter in Fig 22 holds a very taut pose of some sternness; lips are pressed together, legs together, his hand presses rather than rests on the table as if about to rap on it. Because he is not relaxed, one senses impatience, as if this were a very temporary pose, not a long-drawn-out moment. The tightness of the pose recalls the military training corroborated by the medals; despite his years, this man remains confident in his physique and himself.

The lady in Fig 23 is in a pleasantly reflective mood, distracted in the middle of reading. She is lost in her own thoughts with a slight smile on her lips, but the angle of her head seems to suggest wistfulness. Her hand draws attention to her heart and her throat while it plays with the chain of the miniature. Her body is seated but in no sense languorous or relaxed; she is too upright to convey abandonment of a more sensual kind; she turns away from the sail of a distant ship.

22.

23.

In front of a mirror strike suitable poses which would convey the following professions or interests: cleric, teacher, doctor, politician, athlete. Don't rush. Think about each bodily part and its orientation to the viewer. Will your portrait be full- or half-length?

Strike suitable poses which would convey the following states or qualities: parenthood, determination, grace, optimism, authority.

Suggest some other abstract qualities that you feel would be possible to convey by a pose for a portrait: what qualities, for example, would you wish to express about yourself?

BACKGROUND OR ACCESSORIES

What has the sitter chosen to have in his/her portrait besides their own image? Backgrounds, accessories, inscriptions, animals and cupids all hold potentially meaningful information too. For example, an appropriate setting for a writer could be a room with table, ink, pen, books; for an admiral, a stormy seashore. But, as with costume, there is no requirement that these things be actually 'true' or 'normal'. An artist is unlikely to obtain sittings in the midst of battle or speech. A mixture of imaginary and real might be necessary if several points are to be made at once. For example, a crown might be included for monarchy and a conquered dragon for valour, or real children shown with angels who represent dead ones.

Sometimes the symbols or accessories remain a mystery. It can be frustrating not to know or be able to find out the significance of an item, but the achievement is to recognise that something *is* being emphasised for your attention.

Animals, flowers and objects have symbolic meanings. For dictionaries of these and also the traditional attributes of saints and gods see the Bibliography. Here are some of the conventional backgrounds or accessories you may find in portraits:

Baton (40×2 cm approx)	informs you that the holder is a commander in army or navy, not an inferior rank. See Fig 13.
White wand of office (150×1 cm approx)	the holder has a post of responsibility in a royal household, eg. Chamberlain, Steward.
Children	a strong statement about family success; when the survival of children was so insecure a large family was a matter for real pride. It suggested future assurance of the family's status in society. The relative positioning of boys and girls can be interesting.
House and grounds	possession of country estates was a more telling index of one's wealth and breeding than piles of gold. People who had them showed them off as the most potent statement of their achievement.
Coats of arms, crest	symbol of a family's membership of the gentry or aristocracy.
Pillars and/or drapes, Turkey carpets	mostly these have no symbolic meaning, but their visual purpose is to add grandeur and strength to the sitter's image. Turkey carpets were very expensive luxuries.
Purse and Seal	a red cloth drawstring bag, heavily embroidered and brocaded with the royal insignia. Tenure of a royal seal conferred great authority and esteem on a minister, who could authenticate documents with royal authority. See again Fig 10: the Lord Chancellor's seal bag is on the table.
Dogs	signify faithfulness. They suggest either that the sitter has lovable qualities or that, just as the dog is faithful, so is the sitter faithful to his master, monarch or patron. Different breeds of dog reflect variety in the sitter's character: consider the difference between a great Irish wolfhound or a little spaniel.

Exercise on accessories
Do you think it makes a difference to the tone of the portrait whether real or imaginary items or a mixture of both are chosen for inclusion?

COLOUR

Certain colours have symbolic meanings as already suggested. It is helpful to assess whether their use in a portrait is significant. Some symbolic colours are white, black, scarlet, purple, gold and royal blue. The selection of blending or clashing tones is something the artist can deliberately use to create feeling. The history of paint manufacture influences the colours an artist employs: if lime green hasn't been invented, it can't be chosen. Other colours, such as the blue made from lapis lazuli, were expensive and scarce; their use implies opulence.

Artists frequently have a favourite palette, that is, the range of colours they habitually select. For example, Sir Peter Lely liked browns and golds, Sir Thomas Lawrence liked reds and blacks, Romney used a particular pinkish brown for flesh tones.

SIZE AND LOCATION

Very large portraits in which the sitter is bigger than life-size make you stand back and look up, and thus the portrait's effect is to dominate you. For a monarch this is clearly a useful way of expressing relative status. For other sitters, the great size of the work can indicate wealth because the larger the portrait, the more it cost and the larger the room in which it must hang.

Very small portraits (miniatures) can also imply great wealth because the skill of the artist who could produce such exquisite excellence was costly. Miniatures were frequently mounted in elaborately jewelled or enamelled frames, to add to their value. However, the intention is not to dominate the viewer. Rather, they draw one very close in an intimate way, in keeping with their usual purpose of recording affection between sitter and owner of the miniature. Miniatures are small enough to be worn secretly next to the skin, and beautiful enough to be worn openly like a locket, depending on whether the relationship was public knowledge or not. They were ideal for taking on journeys of separation. Photography has made it easy for us to obtain tiny accurate images of just about anyone, and we have largely forgotten the associations of smallness with intimacy and preciousness. Cinemas have made largeness of the human form seem unremarkable too.

24, 25. As illustrated here, these portraits are the same size. In fact one is over 230 times larger than the other: Mountbatten's face is 162.6 cm high.

The majority of portraits are not at the extremes of size, but somewhere around the middle, showing the sitter just smaller than life-size. Remember to judge when you look at them whether these ordinary ones are largish or smallish. Is expense being displayed, or economy? If the portrait is in the rather neutral surroundings of a gallery, try to estimate what sort of room it would originally have graced: public sitting-room, private bedroom, study. Would it have been the main picture in a room?

Reproductions of portraits in books and postcards or on slides frequently do not specify the size of the original. Often this causes the sort of surprise people experience when seeing the real Mona Lisa – 'But it's *tiny!*' The misconception comes from having seen so many large, bold reproductions on calendars, posters and jigsaws which create a false impression of size.

FRAME

In miniatures, the framing is a way of expressing and adding to the message of 'expensive'. Frames on larger paintings can enhance size and grandeur in the same way. They can also directly indicate the sitter's interests. Look for references such as musical instruments, royal insignia, brushes and so on in the decoration.

MEDIUM

This is again a function of the wealth of whoever commissioned the portrait and the purpose of the portrait. Some techniques are more expensive than others; the emotional flavour varies too. Marble is chillier and more stately than softly worked pinkish brown clay; oils are more glossy and grand than rubbed-in pastels or delicate watercolours.

It is unlikely that, from this introduction alone, you will always be able instantly to identify and understand every pose, outfit, accessory and so on, but this approach shows the value of trying to assess them.

A question often asked is, 'Who decides what in the list of choices about pose or size, the artist or the sitter?' Sometimes, but very infrequently, there are documentary records which help by describing the production of the portrait; for example, we know from Pepys' diary that he hired a gown specially for the occasion, but that the pose (which caused him discomfort) and the deep shadows in the background appear to have been suggested to him. Where there are no records one can only rely on experience and likelihood: there are certainly no strictly agreed principles about who decides what. A self-confident and wealthy sitter might be in a position to dictate certain things to an artist about the desired effect or appearance; alternatively, a much sought-after artist, or one who is producing the portrait free of charge, would also be in a good position to call the tune.

The above has dealt with realistic, or naturalistic, portraits. It is helpful to consider two other types where the same scheme of assessment works but on a slightly different basis.

CARICATURES AND ABSTRACTS

In caricatures, abstracts or other distorted, 'non-photographic' style likenesses, we are shown the sitter through a blatantly interposed pair of spectacles: those of the artist. We are given the artist's version of the sitter, for good or ill. Without wishing to be unduly complicated, this could mean looking at what an artist has said about a person's own view of himself.

In the past, caricaturists have often felt constrained to defend their work, and a usual defence is that they are producing portraits as valid as those by professional portrait artists. Instead of altering the image to improve (flatter) it, they are making bold other qualities by which the sitter is recognised.

Thus a caricature can be decoded in just the same way as more polite forms of portraiture, by observing and evaluating the decisions made by the artist – for instance, to exaggerate physical characteristics such as thinness or big ears, or qualities such as slyness. Caricaturists and cartoonists are useful to the historian in that their popularity with contemporary audiences often indicates how the artist was crystallising something generally felt. Obviously, though, caricature is not showing the 'true' appearance of the person, just as figurative portraits often do not.

A consequence of the invention of cheap and reliable photography was that for many artists, there was no longer much point in trying to create portraits in which a realistic likeness of the sitter was important. Instead, they could attempt to capture something about the person which was not their outward features: their personality, character or aura. There was therefore a movement towards impressionist and abstract portraits. When looking at abstract portraits one has again to identify the decisions the artist has made about size, medium, surface texture and colours as above. But now shape, and the relationship of some shapes to others, and the relationship of colours to shapes are things that can be added to the checklist. It has been

demonstrated that to look profitably at naturalistic portraits requires a little effort on the part of the viewer; abstract portraits require the same attempt to involve yourself with the choices made. It only seems harder because the human face and figure are not instantly 'given' to the viewer.

26. The angularity of the drawing emphasises the eccentric angularity of the sitter.

Exercise on caricatures and abstracts

What might be the comments implied about the sitters in these two images?

If you were an artist working in an abstract mode, how would you present states or qualities such as parenthood, determination, grace, optimism, authority?

Does a portrait have to show the exterior of someone accurately to be a good portrait? What constitutes a 'good' portrait?

27.

28.

GROUP PORTRAITS

If there is more than one sitter there is an additional layer of content to be looked for. Sitters should still be individually decodable, but additionally, their relationship to each other should be made clear by the artist: for example, who dominates the group? Are people shown as lovers, family, professional contacts, master and servant or teacher and pupil? The artist will want to demonstrate his skill in accomplishing this, and, in practical terms, to prevent the sitters looking like a row of individual dummies and the portrait being dull. See Fig 41 for an example of a group composition.

Some of the ways of demonstrating relationship are listed below:

Location	sitters nearest the centre of the group, highest up or nearest the front command the attention, especially if they are isolated from the surrounding background as much as possible.
Proximity	how close sitters are to each other indicates their degree of acquaintance; body or eye contact is similarly indicative.
Colour	strong blocks of solid colour in a person's outfit, particularly if contrasting with everyone else's, draw attention to the wearer.
Pose	whether faces and eyes are turned directly to each other or away can be an index of affection; similarly heads turned gently to the predominating figure, or the use of tense or relaxed postures, draw attention to the central presence.

Exercise on group portraits

Study these two family portraits. What differences are there in the effect of the groupings?

How are the groups arranged to convey the relative status of each individual in them? How do the poses of individuals indicate the personal characteristics of each?

29.

30.

Suggested response

In Fig 29 the father is the dominant member, in Fig 30 it is the mother who is dominant.

In Fig 29 the father's figure is taut, bulky, confident, and makes a block of solid colour in the middle of the group. His height and solidity are enhanced by the position of the pillar behind, which visually strengthens him further. By comparison, his wife's face is presented in profile, making her less compelling. She is also much more softly posed sheltering beneath her husband's shoulder, cuddling the child and flowers but still upright and poised. The boy stands next to his father in a position to attract the viewer's eye, posed forward and away from the rest so that his image is uncluttered, and his head is emphasised by the bold lighting and surrounding sky. He is clearly to be shown as masculine and important.

In Fig 30 the mother's figure and face dominate the composition. The pale expanse of her dress and skin form a highlighted area at the front of the picture. Their extent is widened still further by the clothing of the two children. By comparison the colouring of the father's body is made to contrast, but it is half-hidden, slightly inclined from the viewer and from his wife and less imposing. As in Fig 29 however, his physical position as head of the family has traditionally placed him higher than the others.

There is an interesting comparison between the two portraits in the direction of the respective gazes and the nature of the physical contact between them. In Fig 29 everyone is united in looking confidently towards the viewer and standing very close to each other. In Fig 30 the gazes are in different directions and the people much further apart, making them seem more cool and formal.

The illustrations in this chapter have largely been of historic portraits and the implication has been that, whether by artist or by sitter, the image is contrived. However, the same critical approach to what is shown to the viewer will work just as well applied to pictures in newspapers, magazines, television, cinema or wherever the image you see is controlled or edited. It is not only advertising companies who produce loaded images.

Today people still think about their public image and there are a multitude of companies offering help with hair dyeing or grafting, dress and voice re-training and body re-shaping, who promise that the self can be adjusted to convey the ideal message.

DO YOU TRUST THE MESSAGE?

It became clear in the previous chapter that it is hardly wise to decode a portrait and accept uncritically as 'true' everything it appears to say to the viewer. This chapter deals not with obvious fantasy, but with the influence of deliberate flattery or artistic style. Knowing that a source is probably biased but not by how much, or how to test it, doesn't help teachers and pupils. The purpose of this chapter is therefore to discuss some of the ways in which portraits can be biased. The result will *not* be that A's waist can be shown to have been narrowed by x inches or B's dress improved by the addition of y pearls, but that one can locate why, where and how misleading effects might have been introduced. Interestingly, not all of the bias is in the original portrait as produced by the artist. We have to start with the bias in you.

PREJUDICE OF THE VIEWER

Two people looking at the same portrait do not see the same thing and do not, therefore, receive the same message. This is hardly surprising. People severally reading the same book or meeting the same newcomer will all react differently: the book's plot was riveting, obvious, incomplete; the stranger was cynical, trustworthy, handsome. Sometimes people's reactions are directly contradictory. More often they are concurrent, but nevertheless different. How often has something familiar been re-shown to you in a totally different light?

The variety of the response comes from individual personal history. Reading a new book, you bring to it a mass of associations such as 'Fred recommended this; I liked the last book he gave me', 'I read this author before and didn't enjoy it much', or 'I knew a character like this who always made me laugh', thus to some extent preparing your own response before you actually make it. So, when looking at a portrait, it is likely that you will analyse it in terms of your own personal definitions of, say, strength, humour, pride or beauty. Areas of the portrait will also draw different amounts of your attention, depending on whether, for example, you are predisposed to an interest in artistic technique, historic costume, pet animals, or have a strong emotional response to a particular sitter's face.

Old woman or young lady?

31. A famous example of how different people initially see different things in the same image.

Exercises on character
To you, is the Earl of Dorset represented as good-humoured, or sly?

Might it make a difference to an image if it is cropped and part is removed?

32.

It is not hard to introduce pupils to the idea that everyone sees something different by using the analogy of books, strangers and so on. Taken to its logical conclusion, however, does this not mean that there's no point in using portraits (or anything else) because of the infinite variety of possible responses?

A suggested answer would be that we need to be aware that *alone* we cannot extract the fullest possible ideas or information from an object. We need to make a practice of discussing with each other what we see and why we think we see it. After observation of an object and discussion, consensus is the usual result, but it might not be, in which case we have to accept the possibility of an alternative view if properly supported.

SKILL AND STYLE OF THE ARTIST

When looking at a portrait and trying to discern its message, remember that you are not surveying the living sitter. You are looking at some paint on a piece of cloth, some chemicals on paper, some chipped stone, some scratches on a metal plate inked onto paper and so on. You are usually only able to see what the artist put there. Therefore the conclusions that you draw depend very largely on his/her skill in handling the chosen medium.

Some artists are brilliantly skilled at capturing the essence of the sitter. Others will be less sure and have mixed success. Yet others will be amateurishly unreliable. Artists themselves admit to successes and failures, however eminent they are, so be ready to assess their skill; just because a portrait is accorded the honour of public display doesn't mean that it is beyond criticism.

Historically there are good reasons for some artists being more skilled than others, particularly in the 'natural appearance' type of portrait. When portrait art was first establishing itself in England in the early sixteenth century, many native artists had much to learn simply because the art was new, and skills of depicting different textures, facial structure, bodily proportion or perspective had not yet been completely mastered. Examples of their unsophisticated style are frequently seen in Tudor portraits.

33. Sir Jerome Bowes depicted in rather wooden style, by an unknown Tudor artist.

34. Notice the uncomfortable anatomy of this sitter's legs in a portrait by Reynolds.

Immigrant artists from European countries where techniques were more advanced, like Hans Holbein from Germany, or Sir Anthony Van Dyck from Flanders, gradually provided the examples and ideas which improved local competence. But even after techniques were published and understood to a greater or lesser degree by professional artists there were still problems. Sir Joshua Reynolds, by his imaginative range and characterisation one of the greatest English portrait painters, was notoriously bad at figure drawing. Many other portraits taken by a sitter's sister or friend would never claim to be saleable work, but were produced and received in terms of affection and friendly regard.

Here are some useful ways to evaluate the artist's ability to reproduce reliable human likenesses:

■ Study the most difficult parts to paint: face, eyes and skin. Do the eyes look like real living eyes with thoughts reflected in them; or are they simply recognisable as meant to be eyes – right shape, right place, right number – but not somehow living?

■ Does the skin vary in shape, texture and colour around the mouth, eye-sockets, forehead; or is it just 'pink' or 'brown' all over? Hands and hair are other testing areas. Ask yourself whether the image reminds you more of a photograph or of a pub sign.

■ Stand well back to view the whole work in one glance, and look at the proportions of the body and positioning of the limbs. Is the trunk the right size for the legs or head? Do the arms 'join on' at the shoulder, or just hang next to the trunk? Are the shoulders or feet oriented properly, or are they out of true?

■ Look at the remaining parts of the portrait: jewels, lace, fabrics, background, accessories. Sometimes this comparison reveals that the artist was extremely good at these aspects, and ability here excuses lack of it elsewhere. An opulent or sensually exciting portrait can be just as desirable as an accurate likeness.

■ Look for evidence of an artist's personal style or characteristic solutions to the creating of the illusion. For example, Epstein's sculpture produces very rugged, jagged surfaces and deeply incised eye-sockets whilst Nollekens' work is smoother, and pupils are delineated by a delicate line. Gainsborough's paint is put on in an almost impressionist way and his faces look sharply inquisitive and alert; Kneller's sitters are more solidly worked in smooth, flawless pink flesh with heavy-lidded, almond-shaped eyes. There are as many styles of producing impressive portraits as there are styles of handwriting.

The point of considering the artist's technique is to be able to assess how skilful he/she is at rendering an image, and so to encourage you to explore how far you'll accept the image as a good likeness. It doesn't automatically lead you to be able, say, to confront three portraits of one sitter, choose the 'best', and say 'this is what *x* looks like, because this artist appears to have been the most competent of the three'. Why not?

What *is* a reliable likeness of a sitter? Age, health, mood, hairdressers, last night's party, present company, all alter one's appearance even from hour to hour.

Many people have had the experience of seeing a photograph of themselves and being convinced it doesn't look like them. To take Sir Joshua Reynolds again: he was notorious for producing paintings which the sitters rejected as 'unlike', yet friends would congratulate the artist for capturing the essential aura of the person.

As with the issue of everyone seeing something different in a portrait, it looks as if we are approaching chaos where nothing can be deduced about anything, but there is solid ground.

It is important to accept, first, that a person's appearance is a changing, not a finite thing. Secondly, the survival of a portrait may indicate that virtue was seen in it by somebody, which ensured its preservation. Thirdly, in the case of commercially-produced work as opposed to work deriving from love or loyalty, we have an index of what was considered socially acceptable or desirable. Fourthly, (tremendously cheering to pupils and aspiring artists), it is necessary to record every exact detail to catch a likeness of someone.

FLATTERY

Commercial portrait artists hope to please the sitter, for with that pleasure comes the likelihood of payment, rather than rejection, and the possibility of future commissions. ' A pleasing portrait might result from the presentation of the sitter's physique or possessions or implied qualities of personality, or a combination of all. This is why portraits can be so revealing about sitters, showing what they think is important for others to know about them. Some sitters, such as Alfred Tennyson, George Bernard Shaw, Queen Victoria and Thomas Carlyle, for example, were the subjects of a great many portraits, and it is instructive to see which they preferred or disliked and why. You can probably think of instances in your own family album of pictures which satisfy or don't satisfy your own image of yourself. Have you ever worked out why?

Certain physical atrributes such as clear skin, bright eyes, glossy hair, good teeth, straight limbs have remained desirable throughout history. Others have been the subject of changing fashion, such as hair and eye colouring, degree of plumpness, amount of hair to be worn on scalp or face. There is even a degree of fashionable demeanour attributed to certain epochs and types, such as the *joie de vivre* of the Restoration court or the eccentric aggression of punks or the refined languor of the Bloomsburyites. Depending on the contemporary ideal, portrait artists can often be detected gently remoulding sitters towards the desired appearance. One can draw away this veneer of the moment, if one is aware of it, and look at the person underneath. It requires a little concentration. Do your best to compare the portrait's features with the features of living people around you. The sitters would have looked quite normal if alive today; people did not have historically different features reign by reign. Look for physical flattery as the main point of the portrait. For example, in this portrait of Henry Frederick, Prince of Wales,

35. Henry Frederick, Prince of Wales, c1610.

the legs attract most attention; and they have been deliberately coloured brightly, placed centrally and enlarged, porportionate to his trunk, to do this. In his day, possession of a finely-turned leg was a major index of male beauty. Mary Queen of Scots, when portrayed in the white mourning robes worn for the death of her French husband, was the subject of a compliment which compared the whiteness of the skin to that of the linen gauze.

Here are some examples of desirable female looks to be seen in portraits. (There were ideal male images too.) What would today's ideals be?

Elizabethan	absolutely white, almost translucent skin; frequently the lines of the veins were added to suggest this. Blonde curly hair; high forehead with smooth hairline; eyebrows very faint; narrow waist; torso conical in shape. Dignified air.
Restoration	rich brown hair in tumbling ringlets; dark eyes, heavy-lidded, elongated and sleepy-looking; red lips, very pursed; straight noses descending vertically from the forehead; small, plump chins; plump and relaxed body. Sensual air.
Hanoverian	torso very pale, narrow and elongated; eyes more almond-shaped and cool in expression; pale oval faces on long necks; hair piled on top. Noble, controlled air.
Victorian	dark brown hair in ringlets, elaborately pinned; dark eyes; neck tapering smoothly into arms with shoulder line as sloping as possible; body hour-glass-shaped; tiny rounded feet. Devoted or pious expression.

Deformity is usually concealed so completely by portrait artists that you would not notice the fact at all unless you knew of it from another source; for example, Byron's crippled foot and Pope's bent back are not remarked on. The wearing of glasses is often resolved by the merest suggestion of their presence. Skin problems are almost never shown, and there is little documentary evidence about the actual level of their occurrence. One known example is Sir Philip Sidney, who apparently suffered from acne, but this is not shown in his portrait. Scars, birthmarks and moles make only a few appearances.

Sitters can be made to look taller or shorter (whatever the actual size of the work) than reality by careful positioning of the background or accessories, and of the point from which we view them. A sitter looming up against a low horizon looks much taller than against a horizon across the middle of the work. Sitters near a low table or a child or dwarf, or mounted on horses, or against strong uprights such as pillars, look stronger and taller than in surroundings which dominate or flatten them.

PRODUCTION TECHNIQUES

In the heyday of portrait production, the late seventeenth to early nineteenth centuries, the demands on artists who were acknowledged leaders in the field were so great that various strategies

36. Extract from a sheet used with children at Dulwich Picture Gallery, which illustrates the effect of varying the horizon.

The picture is painted at an unusual angle.
(4) DOES Princess Victoria seem to be:
- looking up at you?
- looking straight at you?
- looking down to you?

Where the artist stands makes all the difference to how a picture looks.

A   B   C

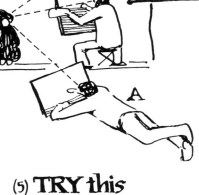

(5) TRY this for yourself.
Stand and sit to draw the same object and see how different it looks.

were devised to make portrait production as efficient and profitable as possible.

One was the use of lay figures, or flexible puppet-sized dolls, which could be dressed in replica costumes so that the artist could proceed with the portrait when appointments with the sitter were inconvenient. Alternatively, the actual costume itself could be lent and worn by a human artist's model.

Much more widespread was the use of drapery painters, by such artists as, for example, Lely and Kneller. Drapery men saved the great man the drudgery of filling in the hair, cravats and costumes of the sitters. Once the face — the most difficult part — had been completed from life and the main outlines of the composition suggested by the master artist, the canvas could be handed over to the drapery artist to finish. The drapery men were very well-respected and a good working partnership was aimed at; they were not regarded as menials. Because the work was brought to them and they didn't have to bother with all the inconvenience of difficult clients, many envied them.

Therefore, be aware that the whole of a portrait was not always painted from life nor need it be the sole handiwork of the artist named on the label. If you are observant you can sometimes spot the extent of different contributions, and any oddness about the length of the neck or orientation of the body may be attributable to this method of production. Naturally, eminent sitters paying for expensive works would expect the work to be entirely by the named artist; lesser sitters could be less commanding.

DUPLICATION OF PORTRAITS

There are two forms to mention: replication of the original, and reproduction in other forms such as photographs or slides.

Replication, or copying

Today, it is easy to reproduce a popular image for wide distribution through photographic and printing technologies. Before the availability of these, there was the same need to replicate images. Portraits of monarchs would need copying, so that many

37. A lay figure of c1740, originally owned by a sculptor. It is approximately 67.5 cm high. As well as these clothes from its original wardrobe, it also has a female outfit.

faithful subjects could own a version. Of Queen Elizabeth I, for example, there are still surviving about two hundred portraits, and there must have been many more in her own day. Yet she only sat for eight portraits. All the copies were produced from the basic eight by workshops of copy artists. Portraits of other eminent persons were also often copied for distribution among family or supporters: government ministers, composers, patrons, poets, great beauties were all potential subjects.

The accuracy of such copies could vary widely. In Elizabeth's time, for example, as long as artists copied the face accurately (templates were available) they could re-create the costume and background largely as they wished. On the other hand, some of Holbein's portraits were copied so accurately, there are disputes about which is the original. It is important for some types of activity, particularly those aiming at the collection of historical data, to establish whether you are looking at the product of an actual meeting between sitter and artist, or at a copy of a copy of a copy of an original. The correct attribution of such portraits could be *either* 'Copy *c*1660 after Van Dyck *c*1640' which would imply that the original was painted *c*1640, and the copy much later, *or* 'Studio of Van Dyck'. This would imply a copy of the highest quality, in circumstances supervised by the artist. He is unlikely to have worked much on it himself, except to add corrective finishing touches to get the right effect.

The cheapest way to publish an image was to have an engraver produce prints. Once the metal plate was etched, copies could be produced quickly and easily. Until the eighteenth century and the demonstration of Hogarth's skill, English engravers were rather limited in ability and Van Dyck, for instance, preferred to use an imported engraver, Wenceslaus Hollar, rather than suffer a botched job. Note that sometimes an engraved reproduction of a painting reverses the image because of the printing process. The correct designation of such an engraving would be: 'engraved by *x* after Sir Artist'.

Prints were cheaply available and were bought by people such as Pepys who would have dearly liked one of Sir Peter Lely's oil portraits of the King's mistress, the beautiful Duchess of Cleveland, but couldn't afford one.

Reproduction

Ideally, this book will lead you to use original portraits on site, but reproductions are useful for preparation and follow-up. The main problems to cause concern are misleading impressions about the size of the original with all that that entails, and inaccurate colour reproduction. This latter can very much alter your perception. Take an original portrait of a sitter in scarlet: if the colour is reproduced slightly towards pink, the flavour becomes more feminine; if towards brown, more drab; if towards purple, more grand. The care with which artists select and mix their colours should lead us to prefer to evaluate the original, wherever possible.

Take care with the use of slide transparencies; they inevitably make paintings appear brighter and richer in colour because of the light projected through them, and may lead to disappointment if the original seems dull by comparison. Sculpture suffers most of all from reproduction in two dimensions, because so much of the sculptor's work is not directly visible.

Reworking

Unkindly, we might call this plagiarism, but the pejorative nature of the term is not really appropriate. Artists have often drawn heavily on the work and ideas of others when making their portraits. If a good idea works, why not borrow it? Alternatively, why not make a comment on a sitter by a direct quotation from another work (think of the quotation of the 'Apollo Belvedere' pose). Robert Walker, who painted Cromwell's state portraits and others in the Parliamentary circle, openly copied Van Dyck, placing his sitters' heads on the posed bodies of Charles I's courtiers: he said 'If I could do better, I wouldn't do Van Dycks'! Naturally, it will not always be easy to assess whether an artist's work is a fresh vision or the reworking of an old idea, but be aware of the possibility, and adopt the precaution of comparing portraits with others on show and in your memory, and you will see this happening more commonly and obviously than you might think.

ALTERATION OF THE PORTRAIT

The appearance, and hence message, of some portraits has changed because of things done to them since they were made. Examine portraits for evidence of any of the following before proceeding to decode:

Inscriptions

The name, date and/or title of sitter or artist may be painted on the canvas or affixed to the frame. These may be wrong, and are often later than the original. There was a great fashion for adding helpful 'facts' to pictures in the eighteenth and nineteenth centuries to aid the memory or increase the value.

Cropping

Cropping is cutting the portrait down to a smaller size. Portraits originally conceived on the grand scale can become inconveniently large when fashion or available house-room changes. Look for items clearly cut in half, or picture edges occurring in odd places, unlikely to represent the original composition. Can you estimate how much larger the original size was? What effect would this have had on the viewer?

Renovation, restoration, conservation

In accurate usage the three terms have separate meanings. All three matter because their application can dramatically alter the appearance of the artefact.

Renovation means improving the appearance of an article so that it is acceptable for use, but without undue concern for preserving the original material of the artefact. Example: re-covering an old chair with new fabric, throwing the old fabric away. In portraits, it could mean painting in or painting out certain details to concur, for instance, with current views on nudity, or re-painting damaged areas wholesale to cover them up and create a better appearance for the portrait; or cropping edges (see above). Sometimes artists themselves change details of their portraits and rework certain parts; this wouldn't be called renovation.

Restoration means repairing something damaged with great care for the historic fabric of the original; for example, repairing the chair fabric rather than throwing it away. Professional restorers nowadays ensure that their work disturbs the historic original as little as possible, and that any additions are documented and totally removable if necessary. Restorers work to a standard of appearance decided in advance. According to policy, they can for example treat areas of missing colour or medium to be indistinguishable from the original, or fill in with something neutral that shows clearly where the boundary between restoration and original is. Restoration policy is an area much argued over. Can you restore something old too much, so that it looks too bright and new?

After studying relatively few portraits it becomes easy to tell whether you are looking at one which has been patched, cleaned or restored or one which has been left totally untouched. Patches often show as slight ridges or seams when you look along the picture surface. Old, uncleaned varnish looks deep yellow and contains ingrained dirt which can best be seen on flesh tones or any impasto (thickly painted) areas, where dirt collects.

Conservation means preventing damage to the portrait and keeping it in ideal conditions for its continued existence as unchanged as possible. Factors such as humidity, temperature, light levels, dust, movement, acidity will all be monitored. Conservation methods should not alter your perception of an artefact, although they are very likely to affect the conditions within which you are allowed to examine it. Lack of conservation would alter the image, because dirt and decay would begin their attack.

THE HANG

It is worth noting that, in places where many portraits are hung together such as public galleries or museums, subtle misconceptions can arise from the way they are grouped. Adults probably understand this, if they think about it, but anyone bringing children into galleries would be well advised to check their understanding.

Most works of art were not produced for public gallery display, but for homes, workplaces, colleges, as love-tokens and so on. The fact that they are all now together in a gallery is really rather peculiar. Furthermore, displays change regularly as objects join the collection.

Many children think of gallery displays as finite things which suddenly came into existence, fully complete, at some time in the past. They need to be reminded of the original circumstances of each portrait, and of the purpose of a collection.

Grouping of portraits, whether by chronology, theme, artist or whatever, can produce a false impression of liaison between the sitters represented, which may not have existed in their own lives.

The apparent age differentials of certain sitters can create misconceptions. Showing Henry VIII aged about twenty next to Anne Boleyn aged about twenty would predispose us to the idea that they were roughly of an age; Henry was in fact considerably older. A separate case is that of sitters in the same picture as their own ancestors, for example Henry VIII painted in 1536 with an image of his father Henry VII, who had died in 1509; or Sir Thomas More shown with five generations of his family.

Experience helps you to pick out the issues mentioned in this chapter more quickly, but be assured that a confidently observant eye will soon reveal them to you if you allow yourself time to look.

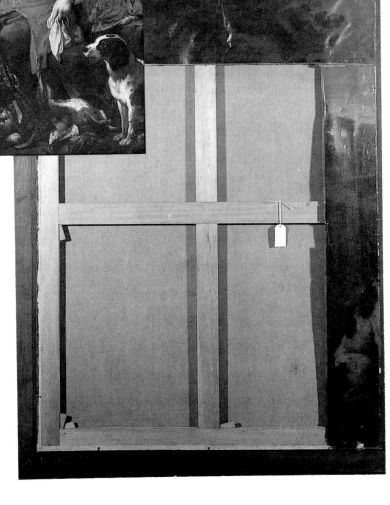

38. Portrait of William Howard, Viscount Andover.

39. Back of the same painting showing how it was reduced by about 38 cm at the top and 25 cm at the side by folding the canvas round a smaller stretcher.

GATHERING MORE CLUES

Portraits are primarily about sitters. However, they are also the repository of many other types of information not easily found elsewhere. The purpose of this chapter is to suggest to you some areas of study you might not have considered but could enjoy pursuing.

MODES OF THOUGHT AND SOCIAL MORES

Portraits provide visual clues to contemporary attitudes to such things as birth and death, what things society finds novel or exotic or beautiful, what activities or events it wishes to record, what it feels about gender, race, age and class. In the same analytical way as before, you can look for the relative roles accorded males, females, children, older people, foreigners, secretaries and so on by their presence or absence, their position within the

40. Maria Maddalena, Grand Duchess of Tuscany, in widow's weeds. This helps date the portrait to 1621 (death of her husband) or later.

portrait hierarchy, their dress and numbers. Portraits can illustrate or celebrate a range of things as broad as the novelty of drinking tea, the authors an educated person admires, the successful growth of the first pineapple in England or pride in a large family.

To take a specific example in more detail: death provides a subject to which many portraits refer. There are paintings of corpses on their death beds, death masks, funeral effigies and tomb effigies, posthumous portraits showing people as if still alive, portraits showing a family's live children together with the dead ones as angels, mothers with stillborn babies, live people contemplating a skull or memento mori (reminder of death), people in mourning dress and miniature portraits in jet settings. Very few of these presentations would be thought seemly today, because our ideas about, and treatment of, death have so changed.

The evidence for different ideas lies exposed in portraits, but the reasons why those ideas were held, or why they are different from today's, will have to be located by further research, in written documents or by reasoned analysis. It is important not to be too simplistic in interpreting pictures, and to point out to pupils examples of attitudes we would today condemn (for instance on race or gender) with reference to their historical context. Harm can be done by making the superficial appearance of something fit an incorrect argument. Children may need reassuring, too, that because historic paintings are on show today, it does not mean that the ideas in them are still current.

AESTHETICS AND TECHNIQUES

Aesthetic awareness is the ability to perceive beauty in, for example, nature or art. This section is about your reaction to portraits as works of art rather than news reports. (It is worth remembering that until the mid-eighteenth century, there was

considerable argument about whether portraits were art or a lowly craft carried out by artisans; after all, the artist only had to copy what he saw rather than create...)

Aesthetic awareness comes into most areas of our lives and our pupils' lives even if we're not artists: in our cookery, furnishings, clothing; in magazines, advertising, typing layout, architecture, design and manufacture of everything from stamps to cola bottles. With portraits you can generally instinctively say 'I do/don't like that'. Then you might go further and say why. A stage further will lead you to an objective level, analysing how an artist has arrived at the effect created, by juxtaposing particular complementary or contrasting tones, gently or strongly lighting particular areas, varying the focus, the texture, the poses, the movement suggested. Composition, scale, definition, handling of the medium (eg. paint or clay) and perspective are other features to examine. When you begin to look at the aesthetic appeal of a portrait you might well find yourself admiring the craftsmanship of a work that otherwise does little to inform or attract you.

41. Notice how the figures in this photograph have been composed to form a strong diagonal line. The effect of this, and of the faces turned towards Victoria in the centre, strengthens her position so that your eye keeps returning to her.

BACKGROUND DETAIL

The setting within which a sitter presents him or herself can be immensely useful to social historians looking for details of customs, tastes in furnishing, or arrangement of furniture. Particularly useful in this respect are the so-called conversation pieces of the eighteenth century. These are small-scale works for often wealthy middle class rather than nobler purchasers, showing them comfortable among the evidence of their worldly success. Often, too, there was an attempt in them to show several people engaging in social activity as if they were not aware of posing, hence their general title. Conversation pieces apart, you will find many other portraits offering views of contemporary lives from Holbein's noble sitters at the time of Henry VIII to views of intellectuals at home.

Furniture, interiors, costumes, grounds

Information on the sorts of textiles used for floors, beds, tables, curtains and hangings, is readily available from portraits but from few other sources given the perishable nature of textiles; not many have survived as complete artefacts or in their original settings. Studying portraits shows, for example, that the Tudors liked to display the pleats of folding or ironing in their hangings and tablecloths, that they often put Turkey carpets on tables rather than floors, and that men wore clothes as decorated and colourful as women.

Views of interiors show the seventeenth and eighteenth century habit of keeping the chairs pushed back to the wall when not in use, the style of glass windows (first diamond-paned, later sashes), the classical design of panelling within rooms to provide attractive dimensions and to incorporate pictures within the design. One can discover the use of pot-plants inside Tudor houses, the introduction of gas-lighting to replace candles, the shape and construction of babies' cots, the changing tastes in pets and the shape and construction of chairs and tables.

Where gardens or grounds are shown, one can often see country pursuits such as hunting or cricket, or the latest architectural style proudly displayed, or the layout of crops or gardens.

Because these things are preserved by the artist incidentally rather than as the main part of the portrait they are likely to be fairly accurate views of household contexts rather than particularly elaborated. In some cases the appearance in portraits of particular items of furniture can fix the date of surviving pieces in a way that cannot otherwise be done.

Exercise on background detail

This small portrait of George II is crammed with information about his life and tastes. The King wears the Star and Riband of the Garter and stands in an anteroom of the new library (by Kent: since demolished, so useful evidence) of St James's Palace. Through the door on the left is a statue of Minerva. Above the door, in the broken pediment, is a bust of his deceased wife, Caroline (d.1737). The giant, rather extraordinary chair is a copy of a design by Gaetano Brunetti (d.1758), published in his *Sixty different sets of ornaments*, 1736. The pug dogs were the favourite pets of the Hanoverian kings. The portrait dates to the late 1730s when the artist enjoyed aristocratic and royal patronage, and was painted for an important family, not for the king.

What statements and/or hypotheses could you now list about the King, working from this portrait?

42.

Clothing, jewellery, make-up, hair

Here again there is evidence of customs or usages which would otherwise go unrecorded. Elizabethan portraits of ladies' skin painted very white and emphasising blue veins corroborate visually the apparent hyperbole of the poets. Early Stuart fashions for wearing large jewels pinned randomly over the hair, or for ear-rings decorated by a trailing lock of hair, or for the wearing of ear-rings by men, can be seen. Sculpture is particularly useful for obtaining back views of hairstyles or dress fastenings.

43. The back view of the bust gives the sitter's name and date and the artist's name in both English and Greek. Anna Seymour Damer was a noted female sculptor.

The tastes and physique of each royal couple in the past have frequently played a commanding role in the formation of contemporary style. Charles I, for instance, wore his moustache brushed upwards, a neat small beard and his hair long, coiled in a love-lock over one shoulder. This is repeated in countless other portraits of men, but is a fashion undiscoverable in contemporary written sources.

44. Bust of Caroline, Princess of Wales, 1814.

26

45. This self-portrait of Hogarth reveals his working clothes, his preliminary work on the canvas in white chalk or paint, and how he would sit down to the easel rather than stand.

Techniques of the artist

Self-portraits provide fascinating information about the studio organisation and equipment of artists. You can see painters' equipment for adjusting scale or lighting; sculptors with scaffolding and clay models; even live models at work.

Examining individual works more closely, one can look for evidence about the construction: chisel marks or fingerprints on sculpture, generous or guarded use of paint on canvas, the colour of the ground used to prime a canvas before it is painted on. Some unfinished portraits offer clues to the amount of work completed at one sitting, or the order in which the artist worked on the sitter's appearance. In photographs, look for details of the typical props of the photographer's studio such as sylvan scenes, Greek vases and so on, or evidence of the lighting or clamps to hold the body still during the plate exposure; blurred bits show where children, animals or vehicles have moved before the lengthy exposure was complete.

46. A Victorian lady dressed as a Greek for the purposes of her photograph; note the photographer's props and backdrop.

What are the caveats to be borne in mind when studying portraits for these types of information? There are many which are probably instinctively obvious to adults, but need listing because children do not have the same discriminatory powers. For instance:

■ pillars and drapes are not typical domestic furnishings, but were added to lend an air of grandeur, dignity or movement to the scene.

■ not everyone is shown wearing their everyday clothes or in real scenes; imaginary presentations are possible.

■ group scenes which represent 'the moment when . . .' such as 'The Death of General Wolfe', 'Watson attacked by the shark', 'Wellington at Waterloo' are often portraits composed by the artist after the event, and are only accurate in so far as the artist has endeavoured to collect and represent real information.

■ some things are difficult to paint as they really are, and may be altered accordingly. In Tudor portraits, for instance, jewels known to be diamonds are often represented as black, rather than transparent or sparkling.

■ many artists copy ideas or 'solutions' from each other, and caution is necessary before saying 'this proves that' even with details of people's homes or clothes. The eighteenth century artist Arthur Devis produced the same fashionable costume for two of his lady sitters, and the same fine classical interior for two separate families. It is unlikely that they *were* the same, but undoubtedly the designs represented fashionable and desirable appearance.

47. *Children in an interior,* by Arthur Devis.

48. Roger Hesketh and his family, by Arthur Devis.

29

PORTRAITS AND THE CURRICULUM

The purpose of this chapter is to suggest some activities which require the pupil to work primarily with the portrait, even if later they turn to label, guidebook and reference work. It deals firstly with ways of relating portraits to specific subjects although many of these activities will operate equally well in more than one curriculum area. The chapter then covers in-school preparation that relates to all subject areas and finishes with some suggestions on the organisation of visits.

The ideas in this chapter can be adapted for a wide variety of age ranges. Infants will be able to understand and enjoy some of the activities whilst teachers may be able to develop some of the suggestions into GCSE coursework units.

49. Re-creating a face.

HISTORY

Improvements in mass literacy, transport, printing and telecommunications mean that people in the western world are accustomed to communicating effectively and quickly by broadcast speech or written word. In general, however, pupils are not accustomed to appreciating the significance of artefacts as a form of communication, and do not develop the skills to analyse this important historical source. Visits to sites are crucial for historians; portraits are something they can usefully learn to employ in discovering about the past.

Extracting historical information from portraits

To help pupils concentrate on one portrait and assess it as fully as possible, you can provide a simple questionnaire (see below) to work through in front of a portrait that either they choose or you specify. The point is to help them generate questions and observations of their own, and so encourage them to record what seems significant to them and not to follow the worksheet too slavishly. One questionnaire is needed for each portrait they do. Different ones are required for single sitters, groups or abstracts because different questions become possible. Questions can be varied to suit or emphasise the particular purpose of the visit. You could design a similar all-purpose questionnaire to help study clothing, backgrounds or frames.

Encourage pupils to spend a long while looking and discussing before they write. Writing should be as succinct as possible; the labour should be in looking and thinking.

50. The important stage: looking and thinking as a prelude to action.

31

Sample questionnaire for natural appearance, single sitters

(Vocabulary to be tailored to pupils.)

Stress that the first person to finish their questionnaires may be doing it wrongly. They need to look more closely. Do anything you can to encourage leisurely observation.

Once pupils are familiar with the approach used in these questionnaires, they should be able to analyse the portraits for themselves without worksheets of any kind, and without guidebooks to tell them what to look for. This skill is of great benefit for life, let alone studying history! Another way to proceed without making written notes is to work in groups. Each group works out its comments on a separate portrait and then presents its findings orally to the rest.

Choose a portrait that really interests you for some reason – perhaps you find the person attractive or puzzling or funny or like the colours. Settle in front of it and think about how it has been assembled. The questions below might help.

Describe the sitter's clothes. (What is the person wearing? Why?)

Describe the sitter's facial expression/mood.

Describe the sitter's pose or gesture. What do these imply?

Do you think the artist has shown the body's proportions well?

Describe the background and accessories. What might these signify?

What medium has the artist used, and what effect does this have?

Has the artist used colours/textures or lighting effects in a special way?

How large is the work? Does this have any effect on you?

Does the frame show any special details?

What is the sitter's name?

What is the artist's name and date?

Why did you choose this portrait?

For group portraits, use the above questions where appropriate but in addition:

Has the artist made any one person or group stand out more than the others? How was this done?

Why do you think the 'important' person has been made to stand out – what is special about him or her?

How do people in the group feel about each other? How can you tell?

For abstract portraits, use the above questions where appropriate plus:

Is it easy or not very easy to tell that this is meant to be a person? If it is hard, how do you know that it *is* a person?

How do the colours tell you about the person?

How do the shapes tell you about the person?

Recording through drawing

Recording information through drawing can be made very much less threatening to the pupil and more efficient if you ensure that pupils only have to draw what is required, and if they understand that they are trying to make an informative drawing rather than great art. Labels and arrows explaining details that are difficult to draw or see are perfectly satisfactory. For example, if you are studying historical costume, get pupils to make separate large drawings of shoes, hat or bodice, rather than a smallish full-length view; otherwise you will find pupils bogged down instantly by the problem of getting the anatomy right. Use whatever is necessary to get round this; for example, mail order catalogues contain hundreds of figures that can be quickly traced for human shapes in or out of the classroom. You will also need to ensure that pupils are really examining the portrait rather than just recording an overall shape from a comfortable distance. Provide some questions to be thought about, for example, on furniture, 'How many different materials is it made from?', 'How are the separate parts fixed together?', 'Is there any decoration?', 'Are any parts difficult to see or hidden?'.

Historical patch studies

Portraits can be used as the starting point for a historical patch study. Choose a sitter and examine the portrait thoroughly for evidence about him/her and the portrait itself, which can include the person's character, clothing, background, and the likely purpose, cost and intended location of the finished portrait; the artist and the medium and fashionable ideals encapsulated in the design. From this point, pupils begin to research outwards to fill in the context which produced the portrait. Some can do research on the character or artist, or costume, or how much the portrait cost relative to other things at the time, or where the media came from, what the house/room it would have hung in looked like, what else was happening nationally at the time, medical knowledge and so on.

Using originals

In order to create awareness of the misleading nature of reproductions for

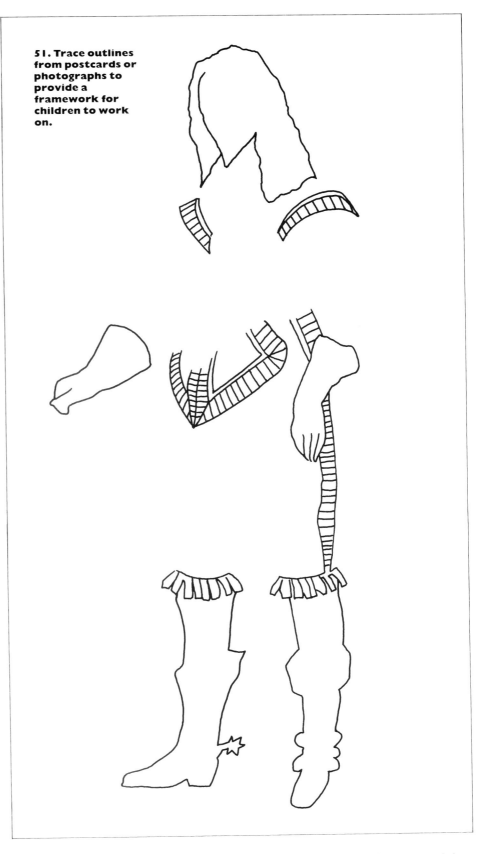

51. Trace outlines from postcards or photographs to provide a framework for children to work on.

historical studies, at school give pupils a variety of reproductions of portraits they will be able to see later on site as originals. Reproductions such as postcards, slides, or photocopies, are ideal. On site, ask them to list as many differences as they can between the original and the reproduction, and then to assess the effect of the differences on their original thoughts about the portrait. Does it matter whether historians use reproductions or not? How far is the portrait 'telling the truth' itself?

The historical function of portraits

To encourage awareness of the important functional nature of portraits in pre-photographic times, (compared to our own assumptions that portraits are merely decorative luxuries), show pupils up to twenty original portraits from before about 1850. Ask them to view each one, analyse it (perhaps using the questionnaire above), and then suggest what particular purpose or incident led to its construction, eg. to record a birth, a new position at court, to publish a statement about something. This should be followed up by a discussion on such things as how and why the function of portraits is different today; why do people keep portraits of their ancestors; why did people in the past often feel a need to have their likeness recorded for posterity?

Evidence for different ideas and attitudes

For older pupils try investigating portraits to examine the hidden agenda of social or political assumptions of the period in which the sitters were recorded. For example, foreign dress can allude to somewhere felt to be particularly mysterious or significant; positioning of individuals in groups reflects status.

Local history

Local history is an area that can profitably involve the study of portraits from nearby houses or museums, particularly if they can be set in their original context so that the wider presentation of a particular family or individual can be studied. There are interesting historical research activities using statistical methods to be found in, say, analysing the origins of a family from the photographers' marks on the backs of an album-full of Victorian photographs, or in the ratio of female to male portraits. The activities in the following paragraph may also help a local study.

Relationship of sitters to their environment or possessions

On certain sites the portraits represent sitters whose possessions or living accommodation is also still on view. The following activities might be used in such instances:

Designing a new portrait: use all the available original material to draw up an impression of the sitter's personal taste and character. Design a new portrait for him/her including what you think might represent a particularly treasured object or view from among those surviving. Remember an appropriate frame and location.

Spot the difference: sometimes the portrait or another source contains a view of a particular room which isn't quite identical to the actual room. Make a list of the similarities and differences and suggest reasons as to why this should have been so. Why was the view recorded?

Building a family tree: if there are several portraits of the same family, construct the family tree and then examine the faces for evidence of family likeness. This will involve some discussion of how fashions for faces changed with different eras.

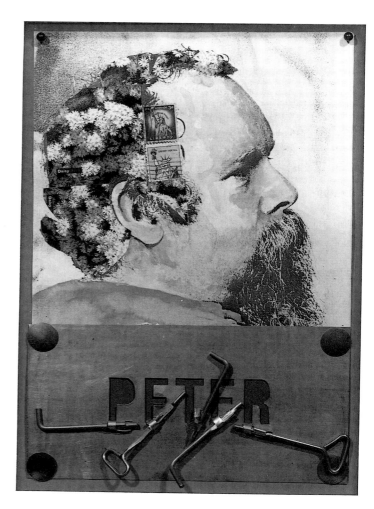

52. This collage portrait by Peter Blake suggests 'Daisy' and 'Liberty', who are the sitter's daughters.

ART

Portraits can be studied both for the information they offer about using particular media, for the creative stimulus to the pupil's own work, and for solutions to particular design problems. If practical work is to be done on site, do check the local regulations governing such things. As a general rule, dry media will be more acceptable than wet ones.

Identity

To study the issue of identity, introduce pupils to the way sitters in portraits can create an identity for themselves by the choice of elements such as clothes, accessories, background, whether these details are real or not. To follow up, pupils can make their own self-portraits, revealing either the truth about themselves or the way they would like to look. For large-scale portraits, lie pupils on large sheets of paper and draw round them. They can collage or paint items on to their outline.

Anamorphic portraits

The Tudors, particularly, had a taste for gimmicky portraits that could only be seen properly from one particular angle; in any other position the image made no sense. Try producing an anamorphosis (see diagram) and then offer up the idea for further exploration and invention.

Mood and character

Besides using appropriate accessories in a portrait, artists can suggest personal qualities by nuances of lighting, colour, size, focus and/or application of the medium. Any portrait, however grand or simple, will incorporate these factors. Pupils can examine and report on these aspects of originals on site before returning to incorporate them in their own work. Make portraits which stress the use of highlights and shade by only working in one colour and white. Study the effect of colour by giving each group of pupils four coloured crayons at random with which to produce portraits of each other. They will have to work out which they think are the strongest or the weakest colours, and where these should appear on the face.

Creating a reaction

Examine some portraits to see what effect the artist is trying to create, and what reaction you are supposed to give. Is it a mental one such as admiration, happiness, sadness, curiosity, revulsion, lust? Or is it even partly physical, to make you step forwards, backwards, view from the side? How is it done? Following this, try to make a portrait which will elicit a response from the viewer. Or take a photograph of yourself and use it as the basis for two new versions, one a flattery and the

53. Children lie on paper and take it in turns to draw round each other to make an outline.

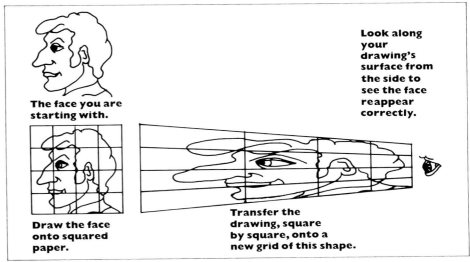

The face you are starting with.

Look along your drawing's surface from the side to see the face reappear correctly.

Draw the face onto squared paper.

Transfer the drawing, square by square, onto a new grid of this shape.

54. How an anamorphic ('changed shape') portrait is made.

other a caricature. What are the most troublesome and the most helpful features of face and body in doing this?

Art appreciation

This means a number of things: the ability to place a portrait in its art-historical context, ie. within a tradition of style and development; the ability to explain the techniques which have led to the production of the work and the degree of the artist's success in using them; the ability to perceive and analyse the appearance of beauty. These elements perhaps seem rather hard for school-age people, but, in fact, pupils from a very young age are not only keen to vociferate whether they do or don't like a portrait, but also to talk about why. The 'why' can be very limited, however, and it would be helpful to extend their ability to express the reasons. A suggested activity in front of original portraits, therefore, is for pupils first to choose

(individually) which portrait they wish to work on, and then to think about such questions as:

Do you like this portrait because of the person/people represented? Why do you like the look of them?

Do you like this portrait because of any of the following? If so, say why for each:

■ the colours used
■ the way the oil/clay/ink/paint has been used
■ the way the portrait has been arranged together with the background (composition)
■ the jokes, references to other stories, reminders of other facts, memories of things in your own life
■ what else?
■ Is there any one particular area of the portrait you particularly admire? If so, why?

Similar questions could cope with portraits a pupil chooses to dislike. After working on this on their own, pupils could present a report on their feelings to the rest of the group.

Abstract portraits often provide the most violent response, frequently negative, and an obstruction to the process of thinking further is the conviction that such portraits are in some way silly, difficult or a 'con'. Group discussion is a good way to begin with these portraits. Ideas to emphasise are that the artist might have wished to indicate the 'inside' of the person, (their mood or character), rather than the outside; and that the artist will have thought carefully about the portrait, and chosen the things he has decided to show. It also helps to encourage pupils to think about how *they* would portray an abstract idea or quality in visual form: how would you paint what a headache feels like? How would you paint what a voice sounds like? How would you paint someone who is famous for being kind?

Colour observation and description

To improve colour observation and description, take some paint manufacturers' colour charts for the pupils to use when you ask them to make a list of all the colours in a particular costume or portrait. This helps them to develop awareness of not only all the different tones of, say, green, but also of where artists use unexpected colours such as grey, olive green or purple on faces.

Posing for the artist

Make some visual comparisons between what facial expressions can be recorded by instant photographs such as big smiles, yawns, and crying, and what can be achieved when the pose has to be held for a painter or sculptor. What are the comparative benefits and disadvantages? Have a look at the work of Hogarth (numerous books available in most libraries) who, before the invention of photography, managed to isolate and draw extremes of expression, from his visual memory. Study and draw examples of different facial expressions from original portraits.

LANGUAGE DEVELOPMENT AND CREATIVE WRITING

There are two possible approaches here: one is studying the actual portrait closely, while the other uses it as the stimulus for a whole range of creative ideas not necessarily linked to the portrait's actual historic identity.

55.

Vocabulary development

Many pupils have a very limited usage of words to denote mood. They will respond with 'This person is sad/happy/cross', but in discussion, it is clear that this is not actually the limit of their own personal experience of emotions and moods. They just don't have words readily accessible to identify them. Build up a vocabulary of a range of 'character' or 'mood' words they might find useful in studying portraits – nouns: pride, optimism, confidence, determination; adjectives: pensive, grandiose, pious, affectionate, strict, anxious, shy, melancholy, solemn, maternal... then visit portraits and seek examples.

A way to help pupils having difficulty seeing different moods is to have them produce speech or thought bubbles for the sitter (obvious abuses possible). Often the words produced do reflect accurately the mood, and you are a stage nearer to being able to discuss it. You can use this stage to warm-up before going on to describe people in continuous prose with extended vocabulary.

If pupils can be split up and can circulate freely ask each to describe a sitter's physical appearance, but not to mention gender, colouring or clothing. Swap descriptions and see if the correct ones can be identified. This exercise can be made even more difficult if only heads and shoulders are allowed.

Portraits as a source for creative writing

This exercise helps accustom pupils to looking for the incident and character content of portraits. Pupils choose a portrait to work on and then imaginatively (as opposed to relying on historical accuracy) bring the character to life. A questionnaire can help, asking such things as:

What is his/her name?
(ie. make one up)
What does his/her voice sound like?
What are his/her movements like?
What is his/her house like?
What is his/her favourite food?
Does he/she have a pet?
Describe a day when your character did all his/her favourite things.

A further extension can be to have two characters worked up, and a description of what happens when they meet.

There is also plenty of scope for writing about, in either verse or prose, what the sitters are thinking about, either in their own lives or in ours.

Exercise on creative writing

Children were shown the picture *The Somerset House Conference, 1604* and invited to explore the apparently mysterious nature of the meeting. Here are three of the stories produced as a result:

'Eleven rich men met in a small room on the top floor of a large house. It was the only room available in the town, it was old and run down and a small tree was growing. Two of the windows were broken and the water ran down the wall. The men tidied it up. They put two new panes in the window (they did not match) and hung a tapestry over the wet patch on the wall. They left the young tree growing in the rotten floorboard because if they pulled it up it would leave a very big hole. They put a carpet over the mouldy table and started the meeting. They opened the window because the smell was too bad. They made plans to rob the bank opposite. They each wrote on a piece of paper what they thought ought to be done. The first man said they ought to throw a rope across to the open window of the bank and climb across. Somebody else entered so they all quickly hid their papers.'

'We all sat round the table on that baking hot September afternoon. All ten of us, all brothers, and our prim and proper father. Why we had to sit there in our big heavy coats I don't know. But our father made us. Of course he took his off to reveal his cool white and blue silk shirt. We were there because we had been naughty. Benjamin and his lot had put graffiti on the new painting in the drawing room. And on top of that all ten of us had performed our pop group 'Oldies' on Sunday, strictly forbidden. Dad found out and so we all had to study the Bible in the summer hols, to learn about the Ten Commandments and the sabbath. But I didn't mind, because 'Oldies' our pop group had a booking that evening at the local disco.'

'The men are sitting around the table waiting for the pigeon to come back with the key to get out of the room. They left the window open for it to come in and they've been waiting so long that the plants are growing through the window. The food is passed under the door and they've been waiting for a year because the key is miles away. Finally the pigeon comes back with the key and when they get out of the door they are met by their wives and children that haven't seen them for a year. The key was lost by a starling who thought it was food. It dropped it on a boat and the boat sailed off before the starling could get it. They were in there in the first place because there was a meeting.'

TEXTILES AND NEEDLEWORK

Portraits are the ideal source for inspiration and information on this subject. Pupils often need help thinking about what they can see, however, otherwise they will see a costume as a flat surface and not as a three-dimensional set of layers. Where figures have padding or other figure-distorting devices, children often think of these as the person's own shape, rather than one induced by the cut or fit of the clothes.

Table carpets, embroidered curtains, cushions, skirts are a complete dictionary of ideas for patterns, repeating or irregular, and can be the focus of fabric design exercises in which old motifs are brought up to date for today's interiors or clothing.

Recognising fabrics

Identification of fabric types is difficult for pupils: make (or they can make) identification kits. On A4 sized pieces of cardboard fix 5cm squares of the sorts of natural fibres used before the nineteenth century: silk, cotton, satin, velvet, leather, lace, linen, brocade, fur, wool. If possible, fix only one corner so that you can see the reverse sides as well. Write the names of the materials alongside, and discuss the relative costs, durability, showiness of each one and its likely use in clothing. You can also talk about decorations such as tassels, embroidery, braid, cutwork, flouncing, padding, ruffling, and the sorts of fastenings available such as buttons, toggles, drawstrings, laces, bows, hooks before the invention of plastics, zips and Velcro. With this preparation the pupils will be well placed to understand what they are looking at when they see the originals.

Designing costumes from study

If you want information accurately collected so that costume can be reproduced at school, you will profit from giving pupils a very small area to record, eg. boots, rather than a whole outfit. Encourage the use of diagrams and sketches explaining the costume rather than drawing a reproduction of the portrait in which the reality of the costume and its construction has not been understood. A useful technique is

56. Elizabeth I, c1592.

57. Costume doll based on the portrait of Elizabeth I.

**58. Princess
Helena and
Princess Louise
with their cousins
in 1859.**

to make as real as possible to the
pupils a need to collect this
information. Younger ones, for
example, can work to a brief: they are
assistants to a costume mistress
working for a theatre which is about to
put on a play set in *x* century.
Information about authentic costume is
sought. They are required to produce
the technical information on fabrics,
colours and construction that she needs.

Compiling historic costumes

To encourage study of historical
costume, show pupils the head-and-
shoulders of a portrait. From collar
detail, hairstyle, jewellery and so on
ask them to locate similar costumes
and produce a description or sketch of
what the rest of the clothing would be
like. Go on to a school-based follow-up
study of underwear, which cannot be
seen.

**59. Replica
costume available
for schools to use
in the Osborne
House education
room.**

DRAMA

A portrait *is* a drama: it has character, meaning, costume, make-up, set, props, lighting; even implied movement sometimes. It does not have sound. Improvisations can spring from looking at any of the above single elements, or by perming combinations. They can be an attempt to penetrate the dramatic tensions of a particular portrait as empathetically as possible, or a springboard for invention.

With regard to the practicalities of actually improvising or performing on site, consider the constraints of large numbers of props or costumes. Clearly it is easier to deal with the absolute minimum. Pupils can sometimes be inhibited by the presence of other members of the public (and vice versa) and the use of a private retreat from which to base the study could be desirable. Check local rulings on the use of music, space and furniture movement well in advance, and before you book.

Bringing characters to life

Portraits may be used to help visualise the characters in a historic text. This is useful particularly if the pupils are not going to see the play staged, but requires a source of portraits of the appropriate period. In front of the portraits pupils examine the individuals shown to discover details of costume. How would the owners move and sit or stand in them? What things seem to be important to them? What make-up and coiffure would be needed to create the right period appearance? Back at school pupils can draw or describe the stage appearance of the play's characters incorporating the historical information they have found out, *and* their own imagination.

Devising an exchange between characters

Both portraits of individuals and of groups represent a moment in a narrative, which is the story of everything that happened up to and beyond the moment captured. Working in numbers to match the number of people in the portrait, pupils can examine the relationships shown in the group, the mood of the individuals, the reason for being portrayed and devise a dramatic presentation to demonstrate what happened either before or after the moment shown.

SCIENCE

Naturally one might encounter portraits of scientists proudly displaying their latest inventions, but more activity-based approaches include:

Causes of pollution and decay

Make a study of the effects of, for example, atmospheric pollutants (on outside statuary, or portraits in smoking rooms) or light or humidity on portraits. Look also for the evidence of badly-prepared paint causing decay. A common example is the use of bitumen by Victorian painters. Bitumen produced a good, rich black colour. Unfortunately, like glass, it never finally solidifies and as it moves it raises great bubbles and fissures in the surface. It can never be repaired.

Following the study, consider the application of the knowledge. What advice could be given or arrangements made to halt damage?

If you can find a restorer or conservator able to talk about or demonstrate the use of X-rays, microscopes, tree rings and chemical paint analysis in their work, further evidence of the ways science and art are interlinked can be demonstrated.

Photographic technique

Study early photographs, in connection with school work on light physics or the pinhole camera; look for evidence of problems with focus and depth of field; observe the different colours, finishes and sizes available; or try to identify different techniques (see Bibliography). Follow up with experimentation if the school has a dark-room; or repeat the earliest attempts at 'drawing with light' on salted paper.

Experimental method

To teach experimental method, use portraits as the subject matter for the development of the sequence hypothesis, method, observation and recording of results, conclusion. For example: test the hypotheses that there are more half-length portraits of women than full-lengths, or that people in the eighteenth century had blue eyes. Remember that any conclusions are probably only valid for your sample, not for the whole genre.

Classification

To teach the use of a key for classification ask pupils to produce a key which would allow other visitors to identify the names of particular sitters without any other labelling. Or draw up a classification which will enable you to identify portraits by particular artists, recording their favourite colour tones, brushwork or way of conveying features.

IN-SCHOOL PREPARATORY ACTIVITIES

Discussing and planning the aim of a visit

The element of surprise is magical and should be cherished. The following suggestions should be read in the light of this:

■ Do the group know where they are going to visit and the origin of the portraits on site, eg. private family portraits, random selection, collection following certain criteria. . ? This helps them to think of possible limitations to the enquiry.

■ Do the pupils understand the nature of the difference between a reproduction and an original? Many children regard original portraits as just more reproductions, particularly if they are already familiar with the image from other sources. They need to talk about how old the originals are, how and when they were produced, (and how the reproductions were made), how they would have arrived in the present location. Quite a lot of children assume Tudor portraits have been dug up from the ground, because they associate age with archaeology.

■ Do the pupils understand the different things that can be gained from an original and a reproduction? (Why bother visiting the original?)

■ What kinds of information do they think the portraits will supply? Some activities could just as well be done from the comfort of the school library ('to see what Charles II looked like') or don't require the portrait so much as the label ('to find out about Charles II's life') or can't actually be fulfilled by portraits anyway ('to find out about the Fire of London'). Remember that if pupils, rightly, say that they will find out about such things as 'costume', they might then need to reflect on how 'true' the information is.

Specialist vocabulary to prepare as appropriate

Artist, sitter, iconography, medium (and specific types: gouache, tempera, etc), bust, etching, engraving, replica, symbol, accessory, pose, gesture, foreground, background, impasto, chiaroscuro, terracotta, alabaster, abstract, caricature, cartoon (two senses: preparatory drawing on paper, eg. by Raphael or Holbein; or picture with caption), cartouche, perspective, proportion, profile, illusion, dimensions, plinth, conservation, composition, daguerrotype, mezzotint, attribution, provenance, Kit Cat size.

Exercises to improve observation skills

Observation of different profiles: in a darkened room, sit a person between a lamp and some paper pinned on the wall so that a shadow of their profile is accurately cast. Draw round the profile of the whole head with a thick black marker, or transfer it to black paper and cut out a silhouette being very careful to keep the exact lines. The identity of the sitter has to be carefully concealed, because the next step is to display the profiles and have pupils guess whose profile is whose. Members of staff make good subjects! (If you charge a fee for guessing and have prizes, this makes an entertaining open-day type activity . . .).

60. Silhouettes of faces can turn into decorations for all sorts of things... compare this idea to all the masks, lions' heads, gods and so on decorating antique furniture, or plasterwork.

Awareness of the differences in individual facial features between people: collect pictures of eyes, or noses, or mouths either by cutting up magazines or taking photographs. Stick them down next to each other. Ask pupils to describe in writing as accurately as they can some of the possible differences between them. The next stage could be to select at random some features and make a face out of them, trace them onto paper and add all the other signposts such as colouring, wrinkles, hair, glasses, freckles, expression lines which make this into an identifiable individual.

Daily alteration of appearance: set up an environment including chair, backdrop and lighting which will remain as nearly constant as possible day after day. Take a Polaroid photograph once a day or once a week of the same face. Take as many as you can in this way – ten at least – and more than one face if possible. Display the results sequentially and observe differences in mood, skin condition, hair condition and so on. Which does the sitter think is the best/worst? Why does he/she choose that one out of so many nearly identical ones? Which do others think is the best or worst?

Range of poses: start with some exercises to explore the sort of bodily positions which suggest the person is still, and ones which suggest they are frozen in the middle of a movement; these latter have weight distributed unevenly or twists in the body, one foot off the ground and so on. What difference would choosing one or the other make to an artist? Are some sorts of pose ('still' or 'moving') more suitable for some sorts of people than others?

Attention to detail: this exercise shows how very small alterations in the body can make a lot of difference to the

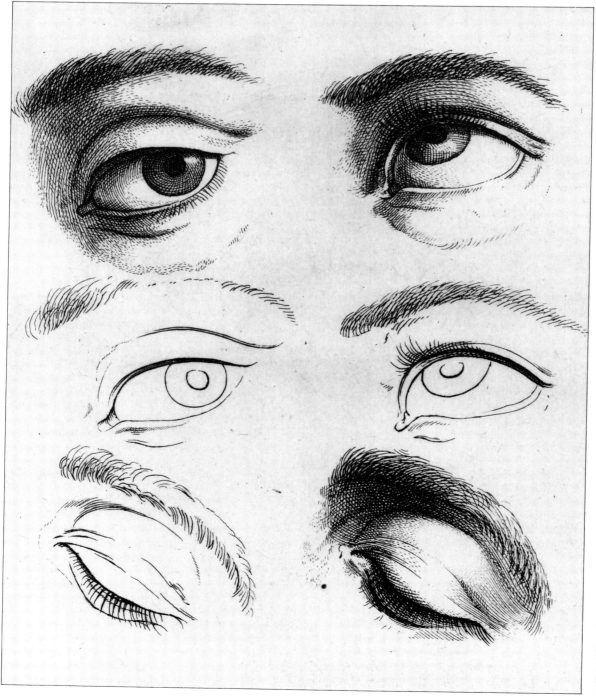

61. Illustration from *Essays on physiognomy designed to promote the knowledge and love of mankind*, by J C Lavater, 1789 ed.

'meaning'. For example, feet: sit on a chair with your feet like a fashion model, a footballer, a shy awkward person, a ballerina, a toddler. . . or hands: hold a cup as if you were a lady, as if you want to warm your hands, as if you were frightened of dropping it and so on. Remember particularly small differences in the spine: hips forward, shoulders dropped forward or held back, upper body drawing away from or towards the viewer, or turned. In the following exercises, keep encouraging pupils to check to see that these little details are remembered.

Choosing suitable poses: get into pairs. Give each person an adjective describing an attitude to be represented by a pose. *Either* A strikes his idea of a suitable pose, B makes adjustments and they present to the group, who discuss it, *or* B models A like clay into an interpretation. Change around and repeat. If you have a Polaroid camera, pupils are helped by being able to see themselves. Depending on the level of the group, increasingly sophisticated ideas can be represented, for example differences in types of 'strength' – physical strength, intellectual strength, economic power, etc.

Alternatively try some poses which represent different professions: cleric, doctor, teacher, author, politician. A sophisticated group could present two alternative views of the same image: a hell-fire priest or a gentle one.

Bringing a picture to life: give out some illustrations of people, one per pupil. Have them study the pose and the apparent nature of the person and then bring that person to life: walk, speak, stand up and sit down in character.

Demonstrating relationships: ask two people to pose together to show the following relationships: parent and child, lovers, pupil and teacher, master and servant, team-mates, sporting opponents, sisters; avoid always choosing inferior/superior relationships.

Planning a group portrait: divide pupils into eights or thereabouts; discuss with them how relationships can be shown by proximity or contact with each other, and how dominance is shown in a group. Give each group a scene to interpret and present as a tableau, for instance, a family picnic or a disco scene, a group of friends having dinner. Have them arrange themselves to show what's happening clearly, and how they relate to or feel about one another. One pupil may be used as 'artist' to check that each person is visible to the viewer, suitably disposed and so on. Present to other groups. A minimum of props could be useful, eg. a table or chair, but the main points should be made intelligible by the pose alone. Follow-up by investigation of original portraits, both of singles and groups.

Variety of facial expression: you need a mirror each and a partner. Just talk to and watch your partner for a while. Notice how the face moves all the time however slightly. What little movements are there? Does your face stop moving when you are asleep?

Now pull some hideous faces. How many muscles can you move in your face, upwards, downwards, sideways, jaw forward, etc? Your face is very flexible, but are the muscles strong? Pull a big face and hold it while someone counts to one or two minutes. Partners watch each other for muscles moving. Conclusion: muscles are flexible, but not very strong.

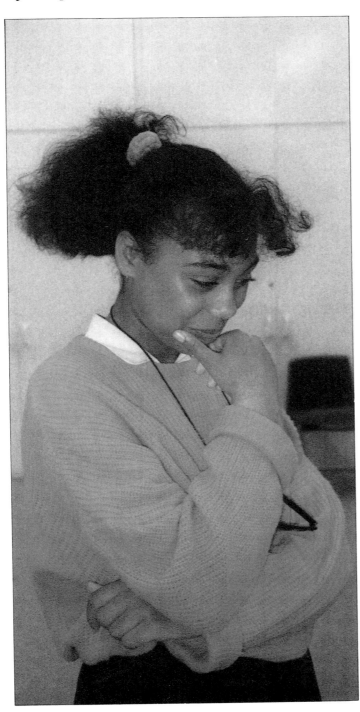

62. Posing to convey the concept 'thoughtfulness'.

Holding an expression: if the face muscles are not strong then an immense variety of holdable expressions come from things that can be controlled such as direction of glance or angle of head. Partners explore the variety, in turn adjusting each other's head and directing the gaze, to see the potential. Explore looking at the 'sitter' from different angles too. Next give them some words to model by just moving each other's glance and head: saucy, thoughtful, haughty, etc.

In the picture: use an old picture frame. Each pupil steps behind it so that only head and shoulders can be seen and strikes an expression. Group discuss what it represents.

Adding accessories: if you have a selection of hats, scarves, glasses, parasols, collars, eye patches, wigs, beards or anything else that could legitimately be included in a head and shoulders view of someone, allow the pupils to make a selection and go behind the frame again, blending the physical constraints, the messages of 'type' from the accessories and the expression.

Follow up with a visit to some original portraits; have partners attempt to mimic expressions from portraits they choose and present to the rest their interpretation of the 'meaning'.

Exercise to improve discussion techniques

Working in pairs or groups is desirable given that two will see more things than one. Discussing what is seen can be more useful than writing it down because you can look at the object simultaneously. The pupils will need training in the idea of discussion, and in generating questions. Failing to see that there is anything to discuss is a major problem.

Give each pupil a largish reproduction of a portrait and ask them to brainstorm fifty questions (or more) they could ask about it. Anything will do:

What are his shoes made of?
How old is he?
Which room is he in?
How much did the ostrich feather cost?
Why is the paint damaged?
Did he have any children?
Why is the picture this big?

The questions do not have to be answerable. The point is to show how two people in front of a portrait could find plenty to talk about. For top scorers, try a refinement. Repeat the exercise with something like a sculptured bust which appears barer of detail. It should reveal many more questions than they would have thought.

If you would like the questions to be answered, you have a lead in to a lesson on research skills. Ask pupils to divide their questions into those that can be answered by looking at the portrait and those that cannot.

PRACTICAL DOS AND DON'TS FOR SITE VISITS

Aims
What do you want your pupils to achieve from a visit? Be brief, and be specific. A successful visit will depend on an aim that can actually be achieved with the material on site. The activity should be controlled by the aim, not the other way round.

Prepare pupils
Check that they know where they are going and why. Can pupils be made responsible for researching and planning the route, timetable, transport, costs and lunch arrangements to their satisfaction?

Booking
Book your group in even when it is not an essential requirement. It is the only way to be sure of access to the area or the exhibits, restrictions on group size, direction of tour route or length of stay.

Timing and length of stay
This obviously will relate to group numbers, travel arrangements, costs and so on, but there are two main points affecting every visit. Firstly, pupils seem to have a super-sensitised awareness at the beginning of the trip and remember in vivid detail the coach trip, the walk, the first view of the site, being checked in, the cloakroom and so on. From there on, memory fades fast, because pupils often move into a passive mode when they are just asked to complete a given task, and there is no need for their personal involvement. Lunch, which recaptures their involvement, is well-remembered. Afternoon activities are recalled very vaguely. So remember to capitalise on the first tremendous burst of receptivity and aim for it to be fed positively, not with administrative detail. Try to devise an activity which requires personal choice or discovery, rather than just conformity.

Secondly, there is a great deal to be said for not filling up the other half of the day with a visit, if it has to be to somewhere convenient and worthwhile but not directly furthering the aim of the main visit. If the pupils experience confusion, exhaustion or boredom or any other negative feelings, not only has the good experience been diminished, but damage has been done to their image of what it is like to visit such places for the future.

Recording techniques — equipment and worksheets

A difficult aspect of site visits can be making written notes. Boards and pencils are awkward even for pupils who can read, write and spell easily. Tailor note-taking requirements carefully, making sure that what is recorded will match the aim of the visit. The use of a camera or tape recorder as a tool for learning might prove interesting and efficient for pupils, if it helps them to look more closely at the object.

Remember to check whether there are any restrictions on the employment of cameras, tape recorders or even drawing by groups.

Worksheets can be very supportive for some children. Points to bear in mind when writing them:

■ If you can provide a framework of choice within which pupils generate and answer their own questions, they will observe more.

■ It will increase the comfort of all concerned if the questions can be done in any order, to distribute pupils rather than keep them in one great group.

■ A certain sort of question appears to encourage observation, but has a negative effect. 'What is she holding?' means that the pupil will answer 'A flower' and move on to the next question, problem solved. The average pupil will not stop to see that 'she' has two heads, a lime green bomber jacket and her feet in a bucket, because these

have been implicitly discounted by The Question. Neither will there be any reflection on the purpose or type of flower. An alternative could be 'Is he/she holding anything? If so, what and why?'

■ Working in pairs or more with an understanding of the value of discussion (rather than copying answers) should help the observational process.

Observation

People naturally stand very close to portraits, wanting to see the details they feel are significant. Encourage also:

■ Standing a good distance away so you can see the whole thing at one glance. The relative values of colours, dramatic effects of lighting or oddness of proportion can only be seen this way.

■ Systematic examination of all parts of the work, not just the bits at eye level. Move if the glazing is reflective. Look at the backs of sculpture.

■ Staring concentratedly at the face, despite an instinctive uneasiness. ·

■ Not touching, particularly sculpture, which always seems to invite it!

Educate for leisure

Finally, if you can avoid totally re-creating classroom conditions on the visit and encourage the feeling that people go to such sites to derive enjoyment, ideas, learning and excitement voluntarily, so much the better!

Of course, not all pupils will thoroughly enjoy the visit. But many will go on to make this type of visit, to historic houses, galleries and sites intermittently throughout the rest of their lives. In doing so, many will also experience that subtle dissatisfaction which comes from patrolling dutifully the designated route without ever stopping or registering any one single article, and consequently not understanding what is there or being stirred by it or fed with ideas.

A successful school visit will train them to see how much excitement they could generate for themselves.

63. Illustration from Facts and faces, being an enquiry into the connection between linear and mental portraiture, with a dissertation on personal and relative beauty, by Thomas Woolnoth, 1854.

Affectation.

RESOURCES AND BIBLIOGRAPHY

WHERE TO FIND PORTRAITS

Your own possessions: family albums or pictures of ancestors.

The things that come through your letterbox: newspaper photographs and cartoons and advertising.

Junk shops: look for the *carte de visite* portrait photographs collected avidly by Victorian ladies, of family or famous; larger scale paired portraits of husbands and wives made from hand coloured photographs.

Local public buildings: schools, libraries, municipal buildings; statues in parks and streets.

Local collections: museums, art galleries.

Historic houses or sites: in the care of organisations such as English Heritage, the National Trust, the Department of the Environment and other various trusts and private individuals.

Nationally owned collections: the National Gallery, Tate Gallery, National Maritime Museum, the Imperial War Museum, the National Army Museum, the Victoria and Albert Museum and the Science Museum, for example, all have portraits on show.

The National Portrait Gallery, London: exists to collect portraits which represent famous British people. The range of artistic ability on show is wide because the prime concern is for the representation of the sitter rather than the ability of the artist. There are also permanent regional displays at Montacute House (Somerset), Beningbrough Hall (Yorks), Gawthorpe Hall (Lancs), Lyme Hall (W Midlands) and Bodelwyddan Castle (Clwyd).

Contact: National Portrait Gallery
St Martin's Place
London WC2H 0HE
Tel: 01-930 1552

Scottish National Portrait Gallery: this gallery holds portraits of famous Scottish men and women from the sixteenth century to modern times and there is also a reference section of over 20,000 engraved portraits and a large collection of photographs of Scottish portraits. A mail order service is available.

Contact: Scottish National Portrait
Gallery
Queen Street
Edinburgh EH2 1JD
Tel: 031-556 8921

BIBLIOGRAPHY

Introductions to, or commentaries on, European portrait art

Davies, A (comp), Ormond, R and Rogers, M (eds), **Dictionary of British portraiture,** 4 vols, Batsford in association with the National Portrait Gallery, 1979. A comprehensive handbook to where the portraits of famous British men and women can be found.

Deighton, E (ed), **Looking into paintings,** The Open University with Faber and Faber and Channel 4, 1985. The second of the four essays, by Alistair Smith, deals with portraits and covers a famous case of rejection, the Sutherland portrait of Churchill.

Jacobs, M, **A guide to European painting,** David and Charles, 1980. Lavishly illustrated survey, helping to set portraiture in its wider context of narrative and other work.

Piper, D, **The English face,** National Portrait Gallery, 1978. An excellent chronological survey which deals with the differing influences of fashion, ideas, personalities and artists on the development of portraiture from medieval effigies to the present. Useful bibliography.

Simon, R, **The portrait in Britain and America: with a biographical dictionary of portrait painters, 1680-1914,** Oxford, 1987. Contains useful essays surveying changing portrait styles, and a very valuable one on the significance and use of certain poses.

Walker, J, **Portraits: 5000 years,** Abrams, New York, 1983. An expansive chronological survey ranging right across the Western world from 3100 BC Egypt to modern Europe and America. Lavishly illustrated.

Techniques, media and genres

Coe, B and Hawarth-Booth, M, **A guide to early photographic processes,** V & A and Hartwood Press, 1983. Well-illustrated and helpful introduction to different techniques and how to spot examples.

Fairbairn, L (comp), **Paint and painting,** The Tate Gallery, 1983 (exhibition catalogue). Excellent description of paint ingredients; chart of colours available to artists at different periods.

Feaver, W, **Masters of caricature from Hogarth and Gillray to Scarfe and Levine,** Weidenfeld, 1981.

Gunnis, R, **A dictionary of British sculpture 1660-1851,** The Abbey Library, revised ed 1978.

Kemp, B, **English church monuments,** Batsford, 1980. Includes brasses. NB Many of these would be regarded as effigies rather than portraits.

McKechnie, S, **British silhouette artists and their work 1760-1860,** Sotheby Parke Bernet, 1978.

Murdoch, J, Murrell, J, Noon, P J and Strong, R, **The English miniature,** Yale University Press, 1981. Clear introduction to the techniques and works of different artists. Beautifully illustrated.

Praz, M, **Conversation pieces: a study of the informal group portrait in Europe and America,** Methuen, 1971. A wonderful insight into the immense amount of social detail these pictures yield.

Stevenson, S, **A face for any occasion,** Scottish National Portrait Gallery, 1976. How engraved portraits relate to the original paintings; reveals how artists worked on the appearance of the sitter or adapted each other's ideas.

General reference works for western art
Murray, P and L, **A dictionary of art and artists,** Penguin, revised ed 1968.

Osborne, H (ed), **The Oxford companion to art,** Clarendon Press, 1970. Entries on artists, styles, techniques and collections.

Human behaviour and appearance
Morris, D, **Manwatching,** Jonathan Cape, 1977. 'A field guide to human behaviour', as viewed and interpreted for its symbolic content. Included here as an entertaining and thought-provoking introduction to body language.

Stephen, Sir L and Lee, Sir S, **Dictionary of national biography** vols I-XXI plus supplements, Oxford University Press, many reprints since 1917. The standard reference work for checking up on who did what and where to find out more about them. May help you to relate dated portraits to a particular phase of the sitter's life.

Schickel, R, **Striking poses: photographs from the Kobal collection,** Pavilion Books, 1987. Large bright photographs of the 1950s, very useful for discussing body language. Also, what makes these poses so distinctively belong to one particular era?

Uden, G, **They looked like this,** Blackwell, 1965. 'An assembly of authentic word-portraits of men and women in English History and Literature over 1900 years'.

Symbolism, mottoes and heraldry
Farmer, D H, **The Oxford dictionary of saints,** Oxford University Press, 1987. Describes the lives of the saints and includes appendices listing their principal iconographical emblems, patronages, etc.

Friar, S (ed), **A new dictionary of heraldry,** Alphabooks, A and C Black, 1987.

Hall, J, **Hall's dictionary of subjects and symbols in art,** John Murray, 1982. Handy references to the meanings of certain common symbols, attributes of classical mythological figures, saints, etc.

Pine, L G, **A dictionary of mottoes,** Routledge and Kegan Paul, 1983. Many sitters want to display their family mottoes; this translates them.

Studies of particular pictures
Cox, A, **Sir Henry Unton: Elizabethan gentleman,** Cambridge University Press, 1982. An inspiring example of how one portrait can yield an enormous amount of historical information; written as a secondary school textbook but of value to all.

Ollard, R, **The image of the king: Charles I and Charles II,** Hodder and Stoughton, 1979. Study of how the political presentation of these two kings involved the arts.

Russell, J, **The Field of the Cloth of Gold: men and manners in 1520,** Routledge and Kegan Paul, 1969. The famous picture of this event (in the Royal Collection) yields much information about the preparation and development of the meeting.

History of interiors
Girouard, **Life in the English country house: a social and architectural history,** Penguin, 1980. Helpful insights into why furniture was made, arranged and used as it was; also puts portraits into the context of the homes that would have been their first sites.

Thornton, P, **Authentic decor: the domestic interior, 1620-1920,** Weidenfeld and Nicolson, 1984. Views of interiors from contemporary paintings and drawings, helping to show in more detail the settings of portraits and details of homes.

History of costume, hair and make-up
Corson, D, **Fashions in hair,** Peter Owen, 1965.

In the series **Costume accessories,** ed A. Ribeiro, Batsford have published (1982 on):
Swan, J, **Shoes**
Clark, F, **Hats**
Cumming, V, **Gloves**
Scarisbrick, D, **Jewellery**
Alexander, H, **Fans**
Farrell, J, **Umbrellas and parasols**
Mackrell, A, **Shawls, stoles and scarves.**

Ginsburg, M, **Victorian dress in photographs,** Batsford, 1982. Very helpful in learning to spot the details and understand the fashion from a source which can be surprisingly difficult for children.

Gunn, F, **The artificial face: a history of cosmetics,** David and Charles, 1973.

Mansfield, A, **Court, civil and civic costume from 1660 to the present day,** A and C Black, 1980. How to recognise the signs of uniform rather than casual clothing.

Sichel, M, **The costume reference** series, Batsford, 1977-9. Clear line drawings and descriptions, very useful for children. Several volumes:
1. **Roman Britain and the Middle Ages**
2. **Tudors and Elizabethans**
3. **Jacobean, Stuart and Restoration**
4. **The eighteenth century**
5. **Regency**
6. **Victorians**
7. **Edwardians**
8. **1918-39**
9. **1939-50**
10. **Costumes of the classical world**
11. **History of children's costume**
12. **History of women's costume**
13. **History of men's costume**

Taylor, L. **Mourning dress: a costume and social history,** George Allen and Unwin, 1983.

Children's books
Cassin, M, **More than meets the eye: a closer look at paintings in the National Gallery,** National Gallery, 1987. An ideal introduction to looking at paintings for teenage readers, but also useful and engaging for adults. You do not need to be in the National Gallery to use it.

Chapters on the composition and techniques of painting lead on to looking at portraits, landscapes, still-lifes and so on.

Waterfield, G, **Looking at faces,** Wayland, 1982. Excitingly varied selection of portraits, including masks, information about each and an invitation to ponder.

Directories of collections open to the public

English Heritage guide to over 350 historic buildings and monuments, published annually by English Heritage. Available from English Heritage Postal Sales, PO Box 43, Ruislip, Middlesex HA4 0XW.

Historic houses, castles, and gardens open to the public. Contains opening times, admission charges, special attractions and maps.

Museums and art galleries in Great Britain and Ireland. Contains opening times, admission charges and a subject index to collections. Both published annually by British Leisure Publications, Windsor Court, East Grinstead House, East Grinstead, West Sussex RH19 1XA.

The National Trust handbook for members and visitors. Published annually by the National Trust, 36 Queen Anne's Gate, London SW1H 9AS.

SUPPLIERS OF REPRODUCTIONS

Borrowing

Consult your local teachers' resource centre. They may also be able to advise on nearby slide libraries lending commercially. Some universities, for example, have this service.

Buying

Stationers, art shops and print shops often have a wide range of posters and postcards. National collections will sell posters, slides and postcards either over the counter or by mail order. Ask for their lists. Photographs or slides of items not on the standard mail order lists will often also be obtainable by special order, so obtain details of this service too.

The Open University study pack for the course **Looking into paintings** contains a book of the same name, audio cassettes, illustrations and gallery lists. It is available from The Open University, PO Box 188, Walton Hall, Milton Keynes MK7 6DH. Accompanying the series were six Channel Four television programmes, available as three videos. The one on portraits, **Portraits and narratives,** provides a rather jumpy but very thought-provoking introduction to the subject. It would be particularly useful for practical art pupils or older general studies/art appreciation groups. You can purchase the videos (for showing in connection with eduational purposes only) from:

The Guild of Sound and Vision
6 Royce Road
Peterborough PE1 5YB
Tel: 0733 315315

The following companies will supply slide catalogues:

The Slide Centre Ltd
17 Broderick Road
London SW17 7DZ

Tel: 01-223 3457

Woodmansterne Colour Slides Ltd
Watford Business Park
Watford
Hertfordshire WD1 8RD
Tel: 0923 228236

ACKNOWLEDGEMENTS

After several years working with portraits it is hard to remember where all the ideas originally came from and I happily acknowledge the creativity of many colleagues in museums and schools. I would especially like to thank Anne French, Deputy Curator, The Iveagh Bequest, Kenwood; Jennifer Ramkalawon, Archive Assistant, National Portrait Gallery, and Mark Eller, for help in producing this book.

64. Storytelling.